From a Joyful Heart

The Life and Music of R. Alexander Anderson

Scott C. S. Stone

ISLAND HERITAGE
PUBLISHING

Published and distributed by
Island Heritage Publishing

ISBN 0-89610-180-0

Address orders and correspondence to:

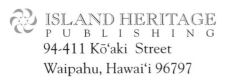
ISLAND HERITAGE
P U B L I S H I N G
94-411 Kō'aki Street
Waipahu, Hawai'i 96797

Telephone: 800-468-2800
          808-564-8800
www.islandheritage.com

Printed in Hong Kong
First edition, first printing, 2003

For Alex and Peggy,
in memoriam

A Note at the Beginning

Robert Alexander Anderson died in Honolulu on Memorial Day 1995, a week short of his 101st birthday. His was a life that spanned a turbulent period, but the facts of his life are no more remarkable than the graces, his longevity no more notable than his achievements. Many a man living half as long and serving half as well would count his life a triumph.

It is, therefore, a brash biographer who sets out to tell Anderson's story, but the temptation to do so is too strong to resist, for the biographer's reward is a closer relationship with the memory of that intelligent and gentle personality. Happily, during his lifetime Anderson's achievements did not go unnoticed, and it is possible to chronicle the salient events of a life well lived. He was, after all, the pied piper of Hawai'i, the man who wrote the songs that came to represent Hawai'i in many parts of the world and whose music is heard today in distant places as well as at home.

Anderson wrote his songs out of love for the islands; as a successful businessman, he never had to write for money. He was a man for whom the word "community" denoted not only a place but also the people of that place and their needs. He served on an astonishing number of boards and commissions that existed to help the community. "Remember I Gave My Aloha" is the title of one of his songs; this book serves as one way for us to remember the many contributions Anderson made to Hawai'i.

I am grateful for the assistance I have had in writing this book. Especially helpful was Pamela Susan Anderson, who has been custodian of Anderson's memorabilia and who was generous with her time and her memories. Her father would be proud. Also helpful were the Anderson sons, Bob, Leith, and Allen. My thanks to musician Bobby Evans for his remarkable knowledge of the Hawai'i music scene and his willingness to share it. Thanks also to archivist Janet Zisk for efforts above and beyond the call of duty, and a special *mahalo* and *aloha* to George Chaplin for his usual optimism and his encouragement. As always, my deep gratitude goes to my wife, Walelu, for accompanying me on yet another literary voyage.

Scott C. S. Stone

At left: Honolulu photographer R.W. Perkins produced this portrait of Alex as a fighter pilot in World War I.

PART ONE

I love to dance and sing of the charms of Hawai'i
And from a joyful heart sing Aloha to you.
In every note I'll tell of the spell of my Islands
For then I know you'll be in love with them too.

—from "Haole Hula"
  by R. Alexander Anderson, 1928

It was not the deep sky of his homeland—a sky so blue it would often resonate in his mind now that he was half a world away. This sky was thin and pale and held a look of menace and the scent of murder. There were killers in this sky, perhaps hiding in those clouds that had been building steadily since dawn. He pushed the nose of his SE-5 down a little, and keeping the wings level, he glanced over at the other three aircraft in C flight as they droned over northern France toward Arras, another in the series of dawn patrols.

He had been here many times before, sometimes up at twelve thousand feet, often lower, always aware that other young men were hunting him, just as he was hunting them. Some thoughts could be kept in the back of the mind as long as there was a job to be done. Even at five thousand feet the air was cool, and he was grateful for the fleece-lined flying boots and the fur-lined outer suit provided by a country not his own. The clothing was British, his aircraft was British, and his squadron was Forty Squadron of the Royal Flying Corps. He'd flown out of a foreign base, Saint Pol, in France. But he had no regrets about the decisions that had brought him here.

His flight had followed the usual landmarks: east along the Saint Pol–Béthune railway where the aircraft began their reach for altitude, over the reservoir near Houdan, and over the red roofs of Bruay. Béthune came up, easily identifiable by the sweeping bend in its canal. C Flight swung south toward Lens and over Vimy Ridge, which was pockmarked from shellfire. Below, he could see Canadian infantry units moving behind a heavy barrage of artillery as they advanced on the German lines.

A sudden, savage lurch and a puff of black smoke brought him fully alert. Hun anti-aircraft guns— for unknown reasons, the pilots called them "Archies"—had spotted C Flight below the cloud cover. The sky began to blossom darkly with exploding shells. He threw the aircraft to one side and put it in a dive, spoiling the gunners' aim and finding safety in another part of the sky.

Ahead he saw a green flare—one aircraft had engine trouble and was turning back. The sky was completely overcast now, and the clouds somehow seemed as faded as the sky had been. He thought they had a melancholy aspect.

Another green flare signaled that a second aircraft was turning for home. He glanced at his watch: 0745. Fifteen more minutes and he and the pilot of the other remaining aircraft could also head for home, wrapping up another in a series of missions that were as dreary as they were dangerous. He began to think of breakfast and was mentally dropping two lumps of sugar in his second cup of coffee when he spotted the enemy planes. He was southeast of Arras. He knew he was in trouble.

The Hun aircraft appeared to be deadly Fokker D VII biplanes, which were capable of flying faster than 125 miles an hour and of climbing

Alex in flying gear beside the SE-5 he flew in combat. The aircraft type was effective, but too often the German planes were better. Still, Alex challenged five of them.

above fifteen thousand feet. His own SE-5, a product of the Royal Aircraft Factory at Farnsborough, was the favorite airplane of the Royal Flying Corps, but the Fokker was said to be the best aircraft in the skies. The German pilots were well trained.

The Fokkers were coming from the east and were some three thousand feet below him. He looked over to see his fellow pilot begin a maneuver that would bring them around and behind the enemy planes—it was better to choose an angle of attack than wait to be jumped. He looked to his guns. There was a full drum in the Lewis gun mounted on the wing above him, and the Vickers gun on the fuselage in front of him was loaded

The aerial dogfights of World War I were no less explosive than those that came in later wars; the sky seemed filled with hurtling aircraft and screaming engines.

CHAPTER 1

and ready. He took one more sweep of his instrument panel—the air pressure was all right, oil pressure was fine, the engine was running at 1,800 rpms, the altitude was five thousand feet, and the time was 0750.

He banked and put the SE-5 into a screaming dive, feeling the stress on the aircraft. He angled for the Fokker on the right of the formation, dropped above and behind it, and fired a burst. If he did hit it, it was not in a vital spot, for the German lurched the plane into a quick half-roll that took him out of the line of fire.

Now he was level with the other Hun aircraft. He saw his companion fire a burst at another German plane then roll up and away—heading back for base. He thought quickly. If he pulled out now, he, too, could break off the engagement. At that moment one of the Fokkers came at him from behind and to his left at about two hundred yards. He could see the tracer bullets hurtling by, and in a flash of anger and determination he put the plane into a tight turn, pivoting on his left wingtip and then going straight for the German aircraft, firing as he went. For a few seconds the planes were on a collision course, then the German pilot rolled his plane away.

Now the other Fokkers were whirling around him, spiraling and buzzing away only to return and fire again. He dived to shake off the circling and plunging planes. In the confusion he looked for Arras to get his bearings. He finally found it, but just at that moment the bullets hit him. There was a stinging sensation in his back, and a red-hot pain shot through his left knee.

One of the Fokkers was right on his tail, almost close enough to run him down. He jerked his head forward and saw the ground rushing at him at a fantastic speed. The dogfight had started at only two thousand feet, and now the ground seemed to be flying toward him. His plane was not responding. As he plummeted, the aircraft began to pick up speed and the elevators began to function—he leveled off ten feet above the ground.

He landed the plane as gently as he could, but he felt the pressure of his seat belt then a blow to his head as his face smashed into the cowling. For a few minutes he sat there, his head ringing, trying to get control. Still dazed, he unfastened his seat belt and clambered out of the airplane.

When he could focus, he saw fifteen or twenty men in gray green uniforms running toward him. He turned and tried to run despite his damaged knee, realizing that even without the wound he couldn't run fast enough in his heavy flying suit to outrun the Germans, who were now closing in quickly.

He'd gone no more than a dozen steps before two Germans overtook him, one on each side. He had no choice but to stop.

"Verwundet?" asked one of the Germans, an officer. Calling on his prep school German lessons, the American replied, "Ja . . . hier." He pointed to his knee.

"Offizier?"

"Ja. Ober-leutnant."

"Komm." The German officer led him some fifty paces to a dugout, where a German medical orderly examined his knee and painted it with iodine. As the orderly was wrapping a bandage around the knee, another German officer appeared and proceeded to search him. He turned out his pockets, producing a small silver case containing a picture. "Mine mutter," he told the officer, and indicated that other than his ring and wristwatch it was all he was carrying. But in one pocket he had a small compass and a handkerchief. Calmly, he covered the compass with the handkerchief and pulled them out, holding them up to the German in hopes that the officer would see only the handkerchief. The German officer nodded, and he put the compass back with a small thrill of triumph. That compass might prove useful, he thought.

Another German appeared carrying a rifle and ordered him to get up and start walking despite his injured knee, which was now beginning to hurt in earnest. The walk seemed interminable before he was bundled into a horse-drawn wagon, which then slogged down a dirt road. When it stopped, two men reached up to help him from the wagon and carried him down into a trench to a dugout area, where once again he was face to face with a German officer.

The officer addressed him in English. "What are you, Canadian?"

"American."

"So! Are you an officer?"

"Yes, first lieutenant."

"Are you badly wounded? Sit down here and let me see." He realized the German officer was a doctor.

"How long do you think the war will last?" the doctor asked him.

"We're preparing for five years."

"It could never last that long," the doctor said, then dismissed him. "That is all."

He realized then that his journey was just beginning. Moments later he was back in the horse-drawn wagon, bumping toward an uncertain fate, and he lay back to take stock of his situation.

The year was 1918. He was Robert Alexander Anderson of Honolulu, Hawai'i, just twenty-four years old, and he'd been shot down, wounded, and captured. And he was one hell of a long way from home.

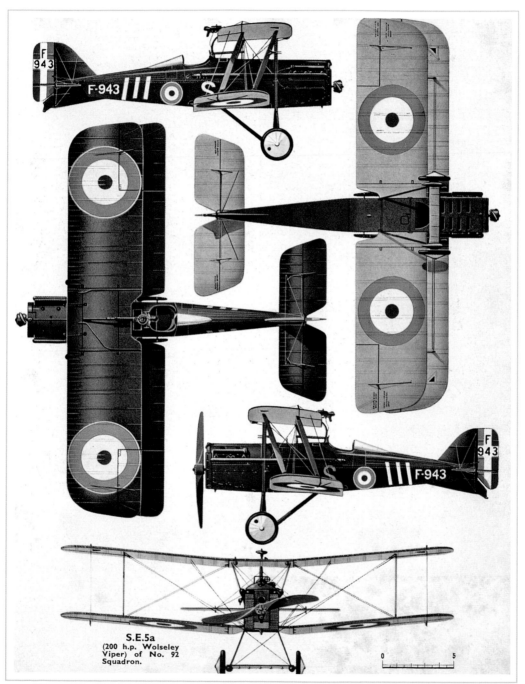

This was Alex's aircraft, the SE-5. Pilots flew in unheated cockpits without oxygen, without communications and without parachutes.

CHAPTER 2

Home, at first, was the cottage where Alex was born on June 6, 1894. It was a temporary residence on Beretania Street near the middle of Honolulu that his parents were living in while awaiting completion of a grand new home at the corner of Beretania and Keʻeaumoku Streets. This fine, two-story residence— so large that it ran all the way back to Kīnaʻu Street—was a wedding present from Alex's maternal grandfather, one of the giants of industry and commerce in Hawaiʻi, Alexander Young.

Young was one of those intrepid Scots afflicted with wanderlust in equal portion to ambition. He seemed to prove the Scottish claim that "Scotland's greatest export are Scots." There was little to contradict the saying; the Scots left their homeland to go all over the world, and among their baggage was a fierce desire to get ahead. They bolstered this drive with a sound education and a scientific bent. Young was no exception. Born December 14, 1833, in Blackburn, Lanarkshire, he received a degree in mechanical engineering from the University of Glasgow, then was apprenticed to a Glasgow firm involved in mechanical engineering and machinist pursuits. In 1858 the firm sent him to London to build machinery, and in 1860 London's Anderson and Company sent him to Vancouver Island under a three-year contract to build and operate machinery for a large sawmill at Port Alberni. Still eager to learn, Young sought and won his company's permission to go off to San Francisco to work and study for a year in the Vulcan foundry. A year later he sailed for Hawaiʻi, where he immediately found work as a patternmaker for Honolulu Iron Works.

Young and Hawaiʻi seemed made for each other, and he looked for a way to establish himself in the islands. He saw an opportunity on the island of Hawaiʻi, and with a partner, William Lidgate, he opened a machine shop and foundry in Hilo—the Hilo Iron Works.

This was during the booming sugar era of the late nineteenth century, when sugar had replaced whaling as the primary industry in the islands; yet the sugar machinery was, in Young's eyes, inefficient. He set out to improve the type and quality of the machinery used to extract and process the juice from sugarcane—that very special grass—and soon invented the automatic mill feeder, the exhaust steam superheater, and the furnace for burning bagasse, the dry and pulpy residue left after the juice is extracted from the cane. Young poured much of his earnings back into sugar companies, and for many years he was president of Pepe'ekeo Sugar Company on Hawai'i Island's windswept Hāmākua Coast and vice president of the Waiākea Mill Company in Hilo. He also owned shares of O'ahu's Kahuku Plantation.

In 1887 Young became a naturalized citizen of Hawai'i, and the following year he became a member of the Hawai'i's House of Nobles. In 1889 he served as a member of the Hawai'i's Constitutional Convention, and thereafter he remained prominent in the economic and political affairs of the islands. When Hawai'i's last monarch, Queen Lili'uokalani, was deposed in 1893, Young became minister of the interior in the cabinet of President Sanford B. Dole.

This was Alex's grandfather, a man Alex grew to admire. By the time Alex was five years old, the Republic of Hawai'i had become the Territory of Hawai'i, and Young had begun construction of the famous

Alex's father, Dr. R.W. Anderson, came to Hawai'i from the Mainland and became one of the leading dentists in the Islands.

downtown-Honolulu hotel that bore his name, the Alexander Young Hotel. Completed in 1903, the hotel was a landmark for decades. In 1905 Young bought the Moana Hotel on Waikīkī Beach, and he later purchased the Royal Hawaiian Hotel at Richards and Hotel Streets. Branching into the automobile business, Young and his son-in-law, Conrad Carl Von Hamm, and a few other partners formed the Von Hamm-Young company, which Alex would come to know well.

In 1860 Young had married Ruth Pearce, of Norfolk, England. Among their three sons and six daughters was Susan Alice Young, born January 5, 1867, in Hilo. It was Susan's picture that Alex had in its silver case when he was searched by the German officer. Alex adored his mother.

By all accounts Young was a doting father, and with his Scottish penchant for educating children, he sent his daughter Susan off to Punahou School, an educational magnet for the offspring of the islands' prominent families. He also encouraged her music lessons; later she would do the same for Alex.

Alex's father, also of Scottish ancestry, was Robert Willis Anderson, who was born in New York but grew up in Plainfield, New Jersey. He took a degree in dentistry from Philadelphia Dental College, began his practice, and got married. But when his wife died, Anderson grew restless and boarded a ship for Hawai'i. In Honolulu he perceived a need for good dentists, and he resumed his practice from an office on Alakea Street, near Hotel Street. Before long he was one of the leading dentists in the islands, making frequent trips to serve his patients on the outer islands. He married the former Susan Young, with whom he shared an affinity for music. He was proficient enough on the organ to be asked to play at weddings and church functions, and he composed the "May Waltz" and the "Bicycle Waltz," which were published by a New York City publisher. In their house at Beretania and Ke'eaumoku Streets, Robert and Susan Anderson had an organ on which Alex learned the rudiments of harmony and chord progression from key to key.

So Alex was indebted to both of his talented parents for bringing him up in a musical atmosphere and encouraging his own efforts. Later in life he learned some things about technique and variations from other musicians, but he never had formal training. The lessons he received early on from his parents were enough to launch him, and as it turned out, they were all he needed. Alex may have had a genetic asset from what many would consider an unlikely source—old Alexander Young, the pragmatic businessman and shrewd entrepreneur, wrote poetry. Far from doggerel, it was verse that revealed a true Scots persona; a no-nonsense mind linked to a wild, romantic, Celtic heart. "I believe I inherited poetic ability from my grandfather," Alex wrote.

In 1894—the year Alex was born—America was facing unsettled economic times; strikes were crippling the railroads, and an economic depression was gripping the nation. A month after Alex was born, the Republic of Hawai'i adopted a new constitution, apparently en route to annexation by the United States. It was also the year that August Escoffier created *pêche melba* at London's Savoy Hotel in honor of Madame Nellie Melba, the thirty-three-year-old Australian singing sensation who was getting glowing reviews for her performances at Covent Garden. A couple of decades later, Nellie Melba would figure prominently in Alex's life.

The Anderson home at Beretania and Ke'eaumoku was a rambling island-style structure with a large lanai. Alex's room was on the second floor, near the front of the house. Alex's siblings included a younger sister, Mary Ruth—whom everybody called Ruth—and an older brother, Robert Willis, Jr., who died tragically at age ten from a ruptured appendix. Alex also had a half brother in New Jersey, Francis Ketchum Anderson, from his father's first marriage.

Alex later described his childhood as a slow and easy life; a life lived in an age of innocence and simple pleasures in one of the most beautiful and temperate places in the world. The mighty Pacific served as a playground for swimming and surfing, and there were languorous evenings and long, sunny days that called the young outdoors. With his Northern European ancestry, Alex's light skin was often sunburned, as he spent so much of his time in the sun.

On holidays Alex looked forward to the strolling musicians who came around the house and delighted everyone with their singing and their artistry on 'ukulele and guitar. After each serenade his father would reward the players with money or beer. Another early memory Alex had was of being with his parents on the balcony of 'Iolani Palace when

Dame Nellie Melba was a singing sensation in her day, perhaps the most famous singer in the world. She made a protege of Peggy for three years, but Peggy left her tutelage to marry Alex, a move she never regretted.

the Hawaiian flag was lowered and the American flag was raised, signifying the annexation of Hawai'i to the United States. Only four years old at the time, he was unaware of the poignancy of the moment, unaware that while some were celebrating, others were quietly weeping.

Across the street from the Anderson house were fairly extensive vegetable gardens, most of which were managed by industrious Chinese. Small streams ran through the gardens, results of the farmers' masterful irrigation techniques. Chinese also grew the rice that flourished in a large field across Kīna'u Street, and they kept a goat that Alex found charming. He ventured over frequently to pet it. On Kīna'u Street was a barn in which Dr. Anderson kept his two sorrel horses, and every afternoon men would climb to the attic and drop hay down chutes to feed the horses below. A section of the barn doubled as the clubhouse for what Alex and his friends called the B.A.C.—the Boys Athletic Club—for they all had baseballs, bats, and mitts. Alex developed a strong ability in athletics and honed his body into the remarkable fitness that would stay with him through most of his long and active life.

CHAPTER 3

The wagon that jostled Alex painfully finally stopped at a casualty clearing station. German soldiers with bandaged heads or limbs sat or lay about on benches or stretchers. A doctor approached Alex and asked about his wounds then barked a command to an orderly, who stepped forward with a syringe and gave Alex a shot just above the heart. Alex assumed it was for tetanus. Moments later Alex was given an ordinary baggage tag on which he was instructed to write his name. The German orderly filled in the type and extent of his injuries.

A little while later another German handed him a filthy bowl filled with a thick soup that looked like glue. Alex decided to drink it anyway, having had no food since very early that morning, and he found to his surprise that the soup was delicious. Then he was marched off to the rear of the station, where a small locomotive sat on a narrow-gauge track at the head of a line of boxcars. He was gestured aboard, then he had to limp from car to car until space was found for him. The small train left immediately.

The train soon reached a second aid station, where the prisoners were ordered to get off and wait for another train. While he was waiting, Alex was approached by two German officers who were curious about where he had been shot down. Alex thought they were aviators. Near Arras, he told them, at about 0830. A bullet had gone through his left knee, and there was a lesser wound from a bullet fragment in his back. The officers nodded in understanding.

Alex passed a bitter and restless night on a bed of straw. In the early morning the Germans brought in a wounded Englishman on a stretcher and put it near him; Alex limped over and clasped the man's hand before he was taken away. Soon Alex found himself back on another train, this time on a monotonous journey packed in a fetid boxcar with wounded German soldiers. The journey was finally broken by a stop at a station in a town, where Alex was able to spot a platform sign: Valenciennes. He was served a small portion of an unidentifiable gruel and some ersatz coffee made from acorns and barley, and soon the train was moving again.

Hours passed. When the train stopped again Alex caught sight of British uniforms, and he knew he was among Allied prisoners. A German officer inspected his tag and ordered him out into the street, where a heavy mist fell over a handful of British prisoners and a line of ambulances. A British prisoner helped him into an ambulance.

"Are you all right, sir?" the prisoner asked. Alex was warmed by the sound of an English-speaking voice. "Fine, thanks," he replied. "What time is it, and where are we?"

The answers surprised him: it was midnight, and they were in Belgium.

CHAPTER 4

In Honolulu, Dr. Anderson stared numbly at the letter from the Adjutant General's War Department office:

> Dear Sir,
> I deeply regret to inform you that your son, Lieutenant Robert Alexander Anderson, Air Service, is officially reported as missing in action since August 30, 1918, while serving as a member of the American Expeditionary Forces. I assure you that you will be promptly notified of any further report received regarding Lieutenant Anderson.

The notice was dated October 17, 1918. Dr. Anderson was stunned. He recalled an earlier notice from the Adjutant General's office, dated June 12, 1918, that had made him so proud:

> Dear Sir,
> The Secretary of War desires me to inform you that your son, Private First Class Robert A. Anderson, Aviation Section, Signal Corps, has been appointed First Lieutenant, Aviation Section, Signal Reserve Corps, to rank from May 17, 1918, upon recommendation of the Commanding General, American Expeditionary Forces . . .

Although he was shocked by the report that Alex was missing, Dr. Anderson reacted quickly, contacting the Red Cross to ask for assistance. On October 24 the Red Cross replied:

WAR DEPARTMENT,

THE ADJUTANT GENERAL'S OFFICE,

WASHINGTON.

October 17,1918

Dr. Robert W. Anderson,
1390 Beretanio St.,
Honolulu, T.H., U.S.A.

Dear Sir:-

I deeply regret to inform you that your son,
Lieutenant Robert A Anderson, Air Service, is officially
reported as missing in action since August 30,1918, while
serving as a member of the American Expeditionary Forces.

I assure you that you will be promptly notified
of any further report received regarding Lieutenant Anderson.

Very respectfully,

Wm E Swanson

Adjutant General

R 358
MAC

*This brief letter from the U.S. Adjutant General related that Alex was
missing in action. The family never lost faith in his ultimate return.*

Your cable about Lt. Robert Alexander Anderson has been received. The moment a man has been reported as missing we try to open every avenue by which a search can be made . . . [it may be] that we have information that the young man is a prisoner in Germany. Just as soon as anything of the sort [may be forthcoming] I shall notify you by cable.

Meanwhile, at Forty Squadron in Saint Pol, Alex's squadron mates began inventorying his property, an event that prompted some sad smiles. In addition to the usual clothing and toiletries, Alex had brought with him a bag of golf clubs, a guitar, and an 'ukulele. The gear was sealed and addressed to the Effects Depot, Base Section number one, in Saint Lazaire. There was always hope, but there was very little real expectation that anyone would ever see Alex again. Every man in the squadron knew he courted death each time he lifted off into the skies.

In the early days of the war some pilots went aloft armed with handguns or sporting rifles, but in 1914 and 1915 the concept of an airplane as a weapons system was shared by only a few. On April 1, 1915, a deadly new phase of aviation was initiated by French aviator Roland Garros, who mounted a Hotchkiss machine gun to the fuselage in front of the cockpit of a Morane-Saulnier Type-L monoplane. He bolted steel wedges to his propeller to deflect any bullets that might hit his blades. When he came across a German Albatross observation plane he shot it down in flames. Soon Garros claimed two more victims, then he was shot down himself by the "Archies," the German anti-aircraft batteries. His primitive machine gun arrangement was salvaged by the Germans, who set out to copy it. Soon staff members of Fokker's aircraft company came up with a similar but better arrangement, and the Fokker aircraft became rulers of the skies. The British scrambled to catch up, and by 1917 and 1918 most combat aircraft had attained a greater degree of sophistication.

Still, it was a heroic age. Despite the increasing efficiency of their aircraft, young pilots went aloft to fight two or three miles above the ground without parachutes, without oxygen and wireless communications. Their cockpits were unheated, and their bodies often froze. The wind was hard on aircraft made of steel tubing and fabric. Tactics often had to be made up on the spot. Few pilots really knew how much stress their fragile airplanes could take, and any new maneuver was an adventure in survival. Dr. Anderson knew that

Alex had been trained as well as any of his contemporaries, but he also was well aware of the hazards.

At his home in Honolulu, Alex's parents waited and hoped for the best. His sister, Ruth, took another step—she went to Washington, D.C., to keep a closer eye on anything that might develop regarding her missing brother.

Ruth and Alex had always been close, having shared many good times and good memories. They laughed remembering their rides in their father's automobile, which was one of the first in Hawai'i when Alex was about twelve years old. As Alex recalled, it was "a Curve Dash Oldsmobile. The dashboard, which was curved, came up about knee height. The steering was by a tiller, a rod moving back and forth as you wished to steer. The cranking was with a crank beside the driver so he could sit in the driving seat and reach over the side and turn the crank."

Alex with sister Ruth in 1942; she married Alex's close friend and fellow flying officer, Paul Winslow.

Ruth and Alex went to Punahou together, the school their mother had attended, and Punahou became a part of their lives and traditions, as it did for many island families. One of the finest preparatory schools in the nation, Punahou set standards by which similar schools, and certainly other island schools, were measured. Many islanders who went off to Yale and Harvard and Princeton returned to find they were still categorized by their attendance at Punahou, and that the Punahou connection was as valuable in their social and business lives as a degree from a prestigious mainland college. There was little doubt that Alexander Young's descendants would attend Punahou.

Alex started there in the first grade, in an off-campus location opposite the old Central Union Church on Beretania Street, not far from the governor's home at Washington Place. The next year he moved up to the Punahou campus at Keʻeaumoku and Wilder Streets, and he went there all the way through the eighth grade, after which he was promoted up to the Punahou Academy. He would remember his teachers fondly for the rest of his life—Ada Rice, Mary Persis Winne, Elizabeth Turner, Susan Clark, and Eda M. Arthur. He took four years of French and German, and both languages later proved useful in ways he could not have imagined. His German teacher was Charles Schmutzler. "I liked his teaching," Alex once recalled. "I think he developed a real German accent for us. I mean he gave us a true pronunciation. He was German himself, a rather quiet man. I don't know if you would say he was inspiring, but you knew he knew his business and you responded to it."

Alex also took a lot of math courses, already planning to follow in his grandfather's footsteps and become an engineer. He was encouraged by his math teacher, Ernest Tucker Chase, who voluntarily led an extracurricular class at seven in the morning for interested students. He had three or four students, among them Alex, who met to study college-level math with an idea of going into career fields demanding heavy math backgrounds. Alex appreciated Chase's efforts on behalf of these select students. "He did that because he was interested in giving us the most he could."

Alex was serious about his studies, and he was involved in a number of lively extracurricular activities. He used to laugh about his interest in "wireless" operations that developed in the seventh and eighth grades. Alex and friends Archie Sinclair and Harold Kerr built their own wireless sets and communicated across five or six miles while Alex was on Beretania Street and Kerr was up on Pacific Heights. Their network expanded to include a gentleman in Kalihi and another in the old ice works on Dreier Street. At their eighth-grade graduation the boys stood up on opposite sides of the stage with a transmitter and receivers, "dot-dashing back and forth," as Alex put it. "It made a great impression on the audience."

When he left the eighth grade to move up to the academy, Alex was awarded the school trustees' Loving Cup, a recognition of his scholastic abilities and his extracurricular involvement. It was a precursor of other honors that he would receive throughout his long life.

CHAPTER 5

An ambulance bouncing over slippery cobblestones in the dark streets of Mons delivered Alex to a prison hospital, where he was led through double doors that were guarded by sentries. Soon he was standing, his knee throbbing painfully, waiting for the next move. A sleepy British doctor appeared and welcomed Alex to the hospital, explaining that he was attending the wounded because the German physician was away from the hospital. He wished Alex a comfortable night and went back to bed.

Alex was led across a courtyard and up a flight of steps, which he negotiated with some difficulty and no little pain. His guards brought him down a long, narrow corridor where gaslight threw grotesque shadows onto the white plastered walls. They moved into a chapel where there were a number of cots, most of them filled with sleeping forms. The chapel had a high ceiling and stained-glass windows. Alex was motioned on through the room into a smaller chapel containing nine beds. He was assigned one of the beds at the same time a badly wounded English prisoner was assigned another. Alex himself needed help getting his boots off and drawing his heavy flying suit over his stiffening legs. In spite of the close atmosphere and an unyielding straw mattress, he was asleep in minutes.

He awoke to the voice of a British prisoner who was assigned as orderly. The orderly proffered a bowl of "coffee" and a small piece of black bread, advising Alex that the bread was the day's ration of food. Alex sat up and studied the small chapel. It was of the same configuration as the larger one, but the walls were painted orange and there was a small skylight in the roof. At one end of the room was a tall, narrow window providing the room's only ventilation. On one wall was a crucifix of the Prince of Peace.

He made a closer inspection of the bed on which he had just slept—and immediately he wished he had not. Both the mattress and the coarse blankets were heavily bloodstained. His observations were interrupted by the arrival of a British corporal named Palmer, who was designated as an interpreter. He was a mine of information. Alex and the wounded Englishman, Pearson, listened closely as Corporal Palmer explained about the Belgian Red Cross visits on Thursdays, when "gifts" were distributed. The gifts consisted of two or three packs of cigarettes, ten biscuits, and an article of clothing such as a shirt or pair of socks, or sometimes a pair of slippers with cloth tops and pressed-paper soles. Occasionally there was soap that did not lather, and towels, combs, and toothbrushes. The safety razors were of dubious value; Alex soon learned that they were best used for shaving the unpalatable crusts from the prison hospital bread.

The prisoners could receive parcels, Palmer told them, and they could write home to the extent of four postcards and two letters a month, for which they would be supplied writing materials. Alex had no money, but he was told that he would be allowed to receive small amounts of money from home, and he would receive an additional twenty marks a month while in the hospital. This money could be used to buy food. He quickly found out how far this money would stretch—one day he and some of the other prisoners sent a German orderly out to buy a kilogram of tomatoes and a small bunch of grapes, and it cost them fifteen marks.

Alex noticed stretcher bearers moving in and out of his area, and soon it was his turn to be moved. Out they went, through the door of the chapel and into the main chapel, through a hallway and into the courtyard. Alex tried to observe as much as possible. The building they were in was an E-shaped structure with the chapel at its center. The courtyard they went through was rather bare except for a circle of flowers with a neatly clipped border of green. A short stone wall separated it from another courtyard.

Alex was carried into what looked like a chamber of horrors—a room with three operating tables, two of which were occupied. Other patients sat around on benches, attended by orderlies and a couple of nurses. A doctor walked over and examined Alex's wounds. There were two holes an inch and a half above his left knee where a bullet had entered and tunneled through the flesh, missing the bones of the knee by only an eighth of an inch. There were bullet splinters on his right leg, but the wounds were minor. The wound in his back was minor as well, and the doctor assured Alex that he would recover with proper rest. He was carried back to his cot, and the stretcher bearers picked up the wounded Englishman, Pearson. Pearson was soon brought back, tight and drawn from having his wounds packed and suffering severe pain.

The days passed, and the prisoners divided them into three segments: morning coffee to first soup, first soup to afternoon coffee, and afternoon coffee to evening soup. Time was not reckoned in the classic sense of B.C. or A.D. but in D.C.—days of captivity.

On the fourth day of his captivity Alex felt well enough to walk out into the courtyard. There he met Palmer, who suggested that since he could now walk around, Alex might want to move up to the third floor, where only two of the nine beds were occupied. He was quick to make the move, appreciating the extra space.

The two officers already in the upper room were Scots named Robinson and Drew. In time Pearson was moved up, then they were joined by another Scotsman, a lieutenant in the Royal Navy named Inglis. Soon two British Tank Corps officers, Captain Hore and Lieutenant Harrup, were carried up. Hore had been shot through the hip and had a paralyzed foot from a shattered nerve. Harrup's wounds were even worse—Alex later said that Harrup was literally pumped full of lead; he bled all over his body but he never complained, even when he had to have one of his eyes removed. "I have never seen more splendid courage," Alex wrote.

The men bonded rapidly. Hore, who was from Argentina, told interesting tales of his homeland. Robinson, Drew, and Inglis talked warmly of the Highlands and of trekking in Scotland. Alex spoke of beaches and breezes, of surf and sand, of "those far-off Isles of the Pacific that are dearer to me than any other spot on earth." Sometimes in the evening when the gaslights were turned down the men would sing together. The songs were wistful and dreamy for the most part, but now and then the tempo would get upbeat, and the men would sing the liveliest rags they knew. Alex was a great contributor to these sessions. He had found a battered guitar in the interpreter's room, and he dragged it out and played the accompaniment. The song sessions helped to pass the evenings, but the days continued to be hopelessly long and dreary.

Alex got off a letter to his mother:

Saturday and a letter day. We are allowed 10 lines on Wednesday and a letter of 20 on Saturday. Still in hospital but my wound is practically healed so I'm ready to be sent to an officers' camp . We are treated well here but it should be pleasanter at camp, where there will be more to do. The Red Cross have been very good supplying underwear, shirts, slippers, biscuits, honey, smokes, etc. You can send me parcels through the Red Cross to the above address. Any canned goods, pineapple, etc., would be welcome. Don't send anything very valuable because it may be lost. I live in hopes of hearing from you by Christmas. Tell my friends to write. We're all cheerful and manage to keep light-hearted. We're really fortunate to be alive . . . my chances looked pretty slim in the air. Time's up, love to all.

There was much speculation as to how long they would remain in the Mons hospital; the German officialdom explained that it depended somewhat on the extent of their wounds but also on activity at the front, which could produce more wounded men and a need for more hospital space. If that took place, the men would gradually be moved deeper behind German lines to camps in Germany itself.

One Thursday Alex opened his Red Cross gift parcel and found that he had been lucky enough to receive "a beautiful pink and white striped shirt and a pair of gray knitted socks." But as he soon found out, not all gifts come without a price. One night he was tormented by persistent itching and awoke to find his body covered in red welts. The following night he was able to get into a hot shower, and afterwards when he reached for that beautiful pink-and-white shirt he realized that it was infested with fleas.

The prisoners were visited by a German officer. Palmer warned them in advance that he was an intelligence officer and that they should be careful what they said to him. The officer was extremely polite and cordial, evidently trying to build up a relationship conducive to data gathering. The officer promised to return in a few days with copies of London newspapers, and he kept his promise. Gaping holes in the newspaper showed that it had been heavily censored, but the prisoners were encouraged to see maps that showed the relative positions of the opposing armies—they indicated Allied advances.

The days dragged on. One afternoon the men heard the drone of a single aircraft. Hurrying to the window, they identified it as a Hun, a Fokker of the same type that had downed Alex. They looked and listened until it was gone.

Something began to awaken in Alex. As he said later,

He quickly passed over us and was soon out of hearing but I could not get him out of my thoughts. The sight of him had stirred me as nothing else could have done. He had aroused anew my longings to be back in the game, back with the boys in the squadron. Oh, to get out of this! Away from this endless monotony, back to the happy days. . . . I sat there deep in thought and gazed absently out of the window and into the courtyard below. My eye fell upon the one bright spot that beckoned like an oasis in the desert, the little circular bed of flowers with its lovely clipped border of green. I looked at it for a long time without really seeing what was there. Then the green border took the form of block letter of the alphabet. I became suddenly interested. What was this inscription that some one had considered worthy the patience and labor of setting it out?

I followed the lettering around, searching for a starting point. I found a period, so I began from there to group the letters into words. They were very closely planted, with no word spacing.

"W-o-e-i-n-e-r," I spelled out slowly. German, and the first two words were *Wo einer*. I followed it through. *"Wo einer Wille, da ein Weg."* That was it. Even with my limited knowledge of German I could not mistake its meaning. It fairly shouted its message to me: "Where there's a will, there's a way."

Alex had always led a life of quiet determination. Even in his adolescence he had been an "even keel" sort of a person—not one to become overly excited or demonstrative—yet he would plow ahead with anything he set out to do. Although he was at the opposite end of the spectrum from fanaticism, he was never known to turn aside from a given task. His calm but dogged pursuit of a goal became one of his trademarks, and he brought it to bear on his studies, his music, and all his activities.

Early on he was interested in sports, not for celebrity's fame but simply as a way of keeping fit. He had a marvelous body and he took good care of it. Not small, not big—he would mature at about five feet, seven inches, and never get fat—he was as active physically as he was mentally. Alex loved every minute of his high-school athletic programs. In a mild understatement he once remarked, "I was on the track squad for four years, specializing in low hurdles which I ran in a couple of meets. I was never a star, but an average performer. I enjoyed the associations with my fellow teammates and also felt that the exercise, the training all year round, was of considerable value."

He also played baseball, and he signed on to play football at a time when Punahou had an outstanding football team. "This was," he told an interviewer, "the time of Randolph Hitchcock and Scotty Schuman. I was put in at fullback and from time to time replaced Scotty at quarterback. We were just beginning to use the forward pass in my senior year. And it was a shuffle. I guess you would call it an underhand pass . . . we hadn't mastered the baseball throw up to that point, that came very shortly after."

Alex had an eclectic approach to life—he was interested in almost everything. He was awarded varsity letters in three sports, a result of his commitment to the training and discipline of team athletics. He also was a bit of a ham, and he found himself in front of an audience more than once. He played Duke Frederick in Shakespeare's *As You Like It*, an experience he clearly enjoyed—he described it as "a beautiful production outdoors, near Old School Hall, under a big monkeypod tree." He also seized an opportunity to write for the school publication, the *Oahuan*. "I was editor . . . my senior year. At that time it was a monthly magazine, it wasn't the yearbook. And I would contribute bits of verse. I apparently had a feeling in that direction and it led later to composing songs."

He wrote his first song in 1912, the year he graduated from Punahou. The song is remembered variously as "1912" or "The Class of 1912," and it was adopted as the class song. Alex later described it as "a kind of football type song that I guess was probably a mishmash of all the college songs I had heard gathered into one." Still, it was a beginning.

Alex graduated from Punahou with honors, walking away with a Roll of Honor award for the student who had achieved the best all-around scholastic and athletic records. Alex had the singular honor of receiving his award from the prominent and respected businessman Walter Dillingham.

1912 was an eventful year. The Titanic sank, China became a republic under former Hawai'i resident Dr. Sun Yat-sen, Arizona and New Mexico were admitted to the Union, everybody in Middle Europe seemed to be at war with one another, and Teddy Roosevelt was wounded by a would-be assassin. In Germany, a twenty-two-year-old Dutchman named Anthony Herman Gerard Fokker introduced the Fokker airplane and opened two factories.

1912 was also the year that Alex enrolled at Cornell University, in Ithaca, New York. His experiences at Cornell proved to be nothing less than wonderful. He pursued a degree in mechanical and electrical engineering, following in the footsteps of the renowned Alexander Young. As he had done at Punahou, he excelled academically but still found time for other activities. He joined the Beta Theta chapter of the engineering fraternity Pi Kappa Alpha and participated in fraternity affairs. He also sang in a Presbyterian church choir and took voice lessons, and he expanded his musical horizons further by joining the Mandolin Club.

Playing the mandolin came to him easily. The summer before he went to New York he had bought a mandolin and taught himself to play, so when he tried out for the Mandolin Club at Cornell he was accepted immediately. Suddenly he found himself to be somewhat of a celebrity, for he also could play an instrument few people had ever heard: the Hawaiian steel guitar.

I picked it up just before going to Cornell, right after graduating from Punahou, from Eddie Hutchinson—Edson L. K. Hutchinson. I knew that Cornell had a musical club, glee club and instrumental club, and I thought that would be a novelty, and it was in those days. Guitar played without an amplifier, just the ordinary guitar. I learned from him, oh three or four pieces—"Kalima Waltz" was one, and those old-time waltz pieces are simple things to play.

Eddie came to my house a couple of times a week and gave me steel lessons. We used ordinary guitars, a steel bar and brass picks, no amplification. Right after getting into Cornell I tried out for the Mandolin Club and made it, but then later, on trips—they made trips every Christmas, concert tours—I was put on as a soloist in-between numbers, with the steel guitar. Played in the big Orchestra Hall in Chicago, with about 2,000 people there. This little tone, it sounded like a mosquito you know, without an amplifier. But it was a great novelty and people responded.

Alex formed a Hawaiian-music group with four other Cornell students who were from Hawai'i. The Hawaiian songs Alex played were

the simple slow ones that I could handle. I was really a novice on the guitar but I had learned enough. And then I would sing one or two numbers with the 'ukulele, Hawaiian songs, "On the Beach at Waikīkī" and things like that. When I got to Cornell I started the vocal lessons and sang in the church choir that was conducted by the vocal teacher, Eric Dudley. So that was the only formal music training I had. I studied harmony by myself. Never studied formally. I've learned to write and to arrange music myself by observation and by reading about it, that sort of thing. But I did have four years of piano as a child. That was when I was about eight to twelve, then my mother gave up because I wouldn't practice. Kids were always outside with a ball and bat, waiting.

Each summer Alex made the long trip home to Hawai'i. It was a ten-day trip—four days by train and six days by ship. Christmases were spent with his half brother and an uncle, "the lifesavers," as Alex called them. In spite of his happiness at Cornell, he had a definite twinge of homesickness. One day he put that feeling into a song:

Far, far across the sea, nodding cocoa palms beckon me;
I hear the breakers dashing on the sands at Waikīkī;
I'm coming back again to you, Hawai'i,
Because I love you—don't you understand?
You are my homeland, my Alohaland.

He titled it "Alohaland," and he had no idea it would become his first hit song. He had gone about writing it the same way he would go about writing many of his songs—he moved from an idea or emotion to a title, let the title suggest a rhythm, and let the beat lead on to a melody. Only then would he write the lyrics, and he often let them simmer in his mind for days or weeks, changing and cutting, adding and altering.

His homesickness was manageable, but it taught him an important lesson: Although he might travel and enjoy visiting other places, when it came to spinning out his life he never wanted to be anyplace but Hawai'i. Still, it would be years before he returned to Hawai'i to stay.

In 1916, just before graduation, Alex and a number of other engineering students were interviewed by a representative of Westinghouse Electric, a Pittsburgh, Pennsylvania, manufacturing company. It was a job-placement program that interested Alex, and he did well in the interview. They made him an offer that he immediately accepted. Two months later, after taking a small vacation, he joined the company in Pittsburgh and started in its training program.

For Alex, the most interesting part of the program was monitoring the electrical machinery on the test floor of the plant prior to its being shipped to customers. This was a night-shift job, and he was on duty from 7 p.m. to 7 a.m., with time off at midnight to eat a sandwich. Alex was happy being around the large generators and transformers, and he settled into a pleasant routine of working, learning, and looking to the future. Little did he know that within a year his life would change dramatically, sending him in a direction he had never imagined.

On January 31, 1917, Berlin notified Washington that unrestricted submarine warfare would begin the next day. This prompted the United States to sever relations with Germany on February 3, and on April 6 America declared war on Germany. The "war to end all wars" had extended from Europe to the East and to the Americas, and the nations were choosing sides. While the fires of war raged, the Bolshevik Revolution began in Petrograd under the order of V. I. Lenin, and the Romanov's Winter Palace was stormed.

Alex read about these momentous events day after day, and he soon realized that he wanted to be involved. "A classmate of mine had also come to Pittsburgh," Alex remembered,

> and when the country went to war we said we couldn't let the country go to war without offering our services. We went to this induction place and they took us both in.
>
> We went to Fort Niagara—it was quite cold there. We were divided into companies and took a lot of foot-soldiering drills. Each company was asked if there was anyone who wanted to go for air training. Right away I volunteered.

In June 1917 Alex and his companions received orders that delighted Alex—he was being sent back to Cornell, this time for aviation ground school. He trained at his alma mater through August 1917, when the eight top-ranking students in his class were selected for flight training abroad. He was, as usual, at the top of his class.

Soon he was the SS *Carmania*, which shipped out of Mineola, Long Island, then headed to Halifax to form up a convoy. Everybody aboard was made to understand the ship was bound for Italy, so an ambitious group formed to learn Italian from a dapper young man named Fiorello La Guardia (who would go on to unseat Tammany Hall in 1932, beginning twelve dynamic and colorful years as mayor of New York City). When the ship arrived in Liverpool the Army apparently changed its mind, as the Army is wont to do, and the aviators were ordered to remain in England.

Alex and some of his compatriots ended up at Oxford, where they went through a ground school very similar to the one they had just left at Cornell. They spent two weeks at Grantham Machine Gunnery School, then they moved on to Huntington. At Huntington Alex took four hours of dual instruction before he soloed on a DH 6 (one in a series of marvelous airplanes designed by Geoffrey De Havilland at his drawing board in

Hendon). The weather was so bad at Huntington that it took nearly two months for Alex to accumulate eight hours of qualifying flight time.

Weather was a problem again when Alex was assigned for secondary training at London Colney, near Saint Albans. For three months Alex and his fellow aviators cursed "washout" days, but they finally got in enough qualifying flying time. First Alex flew an Avro, then he moved on to the famous Sopwith Pup, in which he learned aerobatics in a highly maneuverable aircraft with an eighty horsepower engine. He also flew a Spad, by then comfortable and proficient in an airplane.

In April 1918 Alex was assigned to a base in Scotland to complete final aerobatics training and to learn gunnery. He meshed smoothly into the training sessions at Turnberry and Ayr and was excited by simulated aerial combat using cameras instead of guns. Inevitably, there were accidents, and two of Alex's fellow pilots—Bader and Waite—were killed.

In May Alex stood proudly at attention as his wings were pinned on his breast by Major Jeffrey Dwyer, Commanding Officer of U.S. aviation trainees in Great Britain. Alex was designated a first lieutenant in the Aviation Section of the Signal Corps. In July, when it seemed to be raining all over the world, he was ordered to report to the pilot "pool" in France, and on August 1

The daring young men: Alex's instructors at the flying school in Ayr, Scotland.

CHAPTER **6**

he reported to Forty Squadron at Saint Pol, France, for combat duty with the Royal Flying Corps, which soon became the Royal Air Force.

Saint Pol was near the western end of the British forces' lines. Forty Squadron's assignment was to patrol the lines, generally at twelve thousand feet, as cover for the artillery observation planes. Their route covered northern France—including Vimy Ridge, Bruay, and Lens—and it stretched as far south as Amiens. The flights became known as The Dawn Patrols.

Flying over the infantry clashes taking place on the ground, Alex often thought of the carnage below and was profoundly grateful to be an aviator:

> I fell to picturing some of the scenes I knew were being enacted there below, of which the ugly details were so mercifully spared us, and I felt sincerely grateful toward a kindly fate for permitting me to make war on the wing. I felt keen admiration for those who fought on the ground. It was all so easy in the air. It was sport. There was the excitement, the thrill, the pure joy of flying, and above all the knowledge that death would be so sudden, so sure, if it did come. There were no hardships in the life of the aviator. There was only one hideous possibility, which I rarely permitted myself to think of, and that—flames!

Forty Squadron's job was to protect other Allied aircraft flying missions that were observing and reporting on the activity on the ground. "To these machines is assigned the important business of directing our battery fire by telegraph, and they rely largely upon us for defense," Alex wrote.

> The farther we went over Hun-land the farther they toddled along after us, placing implicit confidence in our ability to protect them from any Boche scouts who might be lurking about ready to pounce upon them. They seemed to us ridiculously clumsy and slow, as now and again one of them would roll over on her side to show us her marking circles. For they have a remarkably Hunnish appearance with their overhanging top planes, and wisely take precautions against being shot at by their own scouts.

Life in the air was certainly thrilling, and Alex found the squadron routine pleasant enough. He had time to play a little golf or strum an 'ukulele or guitar with his squadron mates. If he sometimes daydreamed about the surf at Waikīkī, he kept it to himself and went about the business of flying with the same intensity and skill that he brought to bear on everything else.

On a steamy August day in 1918, Alex and a pilot flying another SE-5 jumped a German two-seater aircraft over German territory near Douai. Both pilots made passes, and the German aircraft was shot out of the sky. Each man believed his own pass had brought down the German plane, but it was a moot point since no other pilots had witnessed their kill. It went into the records as an unconfirmed kill. Only days later, on August 28, Alex fell victim to the five Fokkers.

On the morning of the day he was shot down Alex was called, as usual, at 0530. He stopped at the mess for a cup of tea, a hard-boiled egg, and a sandwich, then he went on out to the tarmac to meet his other three companions. The four of them, helmeted and weighted down with heavy flying suits, trudged over to the flight shed where three of their four aircraft were waiting, their propellers turning over as their engines warmed up. Alex's plane was being worked over by mechanics to no avail.

"I hated the thought of being left behind," he wrote. "Now that I was thoroughly awake, it would indeed be disappointing to let the others get off without me." But then the chief mechanic ran up and pointed to a new plane that had been brought in only the night before. Mechanics had worked on it all night, and it was ready to go. C Flight's leader agreed to let Alex fly it. Five minutes later Alex felt the rush of cool air against his cheek and saw the earth falling away as he angled upward in this new aircraft, climbing into that thin, pale sky.

When he made up his mind to escape from the prison hospital, Alex considered three alternatives. First, he could try to make his way through the Hun lines into the no man's land between the lines, then move on toward the Allied positions. The advantage of this was that the distance would be shorter than if he went any other way. The disadvantages were weighty. He would be traversing land heavily occupied by German forces and sparsely populated by Belgians, who, he hoped, would help him if they could.

His second choice would be to walk the entire length of Belgium to the border of Holland. This had the advantage of a larger civilian population that presumably could be drawn on for food and any other necessary aid, and there would be less German occupation forces the farther he got away from the front. The serious obstacle here was the border defense, about which he had heard alarming tales.

His third alternative was an admittedly wild scheme, but if it worked it would be with great success. "Couldn't I steal away with one of the Hun's own planes? I remembered how careless we were at our own airdromes. If conditions were about the same on this side of the lines I was certain I could do it." As difficult as it seemed to be, the scheme stayed in Alex's mind.

Thoughts of escape now occupied his waking moments. He held fast to the idea that he could steal a German aircraft and fly it to freedom:

> Of course, there would be difficulties. It would be a strange machine; I might not be able to find the throttle lever before I was discovered and it was too late. However, I had been in a Hun Albatross scout that we had at the fighting school in Scotland . . . the

more I considered this wild plan of escape the more it appealed to me. Once off the ground I would fly due west and close to the ground, trusting not to meet any Allied planes before reaching the lines. At the first sign of hostilities from the ground I would know that I was over our own lines and would land immediately, permitting myself to be "captured" by the British.

How wonderful it would be to call the squadron, "Hello, Major, this is Anderson," I would announce myself, "Yes, Major, just got back from Hun-land. Brought a young Fokker with me. What shall I do with it?"

In preparation for his escape, Alex found a use for a corncob pipe that had been one of his gifts from the Red Cross. He hollowed out the bowl and placed his small compass in it—the compass he had hidden in his handkerchief when he was first searched. He tamped some tobacco over the compass to secure it.

He began to work on an escape route. He studied the building and courtyard with a British tommy named Ginger, who worked in the cookhouse. Ginger thought he could escape by sliding down a drainpipe from the third floor. But once he reached the ground he would have to go through one of the attached houses that sat opposite the hospital. In one of the houses there were three young girls who often came to their window and waved to the prisoners. Alex began to plot ways of contacting the girls without being seen by the Germans, sensing that the girls would help him if they could. He shared his escape ideas with the other prisoners.

Suddenly, it all came apart. Robinson came in to report that he'd just been told to pack his gear and get ready to move: he was leaving immediately for Germany. In a few minutes the Scot had his bags packed, and with his tam-o'-shanter at a jaunty angle on his head, he said goodbye and walked out through the doors to his escort of guards. Alex never saw him again.

Alex had been counting on Robinson to make an escape attempt with him, and now Robinson was gone. Glumly, he heard the other prisoners advise him to abandon his plans, especially his scheme to steal a German airplane.

Things brightened up for a bit when Red Cross packages began arriving from England. For the first—and, as it turned out, the last—time in Mons, the prisoners had a feast. That night they cooked a feast over a

CHAPTER 7

gas stove in the interpreters' quarters, and it was wonderful—a first course of salmon followed by meat, gravy, and vegetables. They ate so much that every one of them was up later with indigestion, but it was worth it. No one suspected that it would be a farewell banquet.

The feast took place on a Friday night, September 20. The following Sunday, Palmer came to Alex with the news that he'd turned up a pair of shoes for Alex, to replace the paper-soled ones he was now wearing. The shoes, which were real leather, were a personal gift from the man who was in charge of the Belgian Red Cross in Mons and who owned a shoe factory in Brussels. The gift was pure serendipity, for later that day Alex was ordered to leave Mons.

Before he left, Alex shook hands all around. He hid his corncob pipe deep in his pack, put on his new shoes, and got ready to leave. His goodbye to Drew and Inglis was poignant. "Brief though they were," he remembered, "those friendships in the Hun hospital meant much." He hoped that someday the friendships could be renewed.

He stopped to say goodbye to Palmer, who slipped a dozen biscuits into his pack. Then he stepped outside to meet the other prisoners with whom he would march. Their destination was a mystery.

Alex was toughened by the war and his particular circumstances. The hospital fare had been poor, dysentery was prevalent, and his future was now uncertain and likely to be perilous. He was surrounded by enemy soldiers, but he burned to escape, and he found within himself a strength that enhanced his innate determination. He was more determined than ever to take charge of his life, and he found within himself that hard core of toughness he would need to make his escape. He was no sooner out the door of the prison hospital than he began to look for opportunities.

The prisoners were marched through the streets—a party of eight British soldiers, Alex, and an American Army private, a small man Alex knew only as Fleugel. Alex marched with Fleugel at the rear of the small column. The column went through narrow streets and was halted at the headquarters of the Belgian Red Cross. There the Red Cross workers gave them presents—shirts, socks, and some rough underclothing. They also were each given a tin of molasses, two dozen square brown biscuits, and a bag to carry it all in. The Red Cross took down all their names and addresses, and Alex hoped they would notify his parents that he was safe.

The prisoners were marched to a train station, and on the way they passed through crowds of Belgian bystanders. The prisoners could hear the people whispering "prisoners Anglais," which annoyed the little American private. "Américains," he called back, pointing to himself and Alex, and he was rewarded with a little buzz of excitement among the Belgians.

At the train station the prisoners were marched to the last car of a waiting locomotive. They were hustled aboard and locked in. Alex considered the possibilities for escaping from the train but concluded that he had to wait—there were just too many Germans too close by.

At three in the afternoon the train pulled out of the station and began a journey across a flat countryside of green fields and cultivated plots. Here and there Alex could see red-roofed farmhouses and sometimes clusters of houses that made up a village. There was, he knew, only one large city in Belgium, and that was Brussels.

The prisoners were ordered out of the train at the next stop, a village called Péruwelz. As they walked through the village Alex's new shoes began to pinch, and he developed a raging thirst. They climbed a steep hill to reach another village. Alex thought of how the German prisoners were treated in England—a damned good life compared to this, he thought.

They stopped for a rest in the village. While the German guards were treated to beer a Belgian woman hurried over to the prisoners, a bottle in one hand and a glass in the other. She glanced nervously at the guards but then began pouring beer into the glass and offering it to the prisoners, who crowded forward eagerly. They all got a drink, and nothing, to Alex's mind, before or after, tasted as good. Moments later they heard a strange, thumping sound, and looked to find an old woman in wooden shoes clumping toward them, holding up her apron. When she reached the prisoners she lowered her apron; it was full of apples and pears. There was a sudden shout and the old woman hastened away—the guards were ringing the prisoners again because a staff car with German officers was passing by. But in a little while the Belgians crowded forward again, trying to get news of the war. Some of them asked Alex how many Americans were already in France. "Un mois—trois cent mille hommes," he told them: one month, three hundred thousand men. This seemed to cheer the Belgians immensely.

The guards soon roused the prisoners, and the march continued. They entered a town, the column marching through the streets at the usual pace, but Alex began to detect an air of uncertainty among the German guards. Their uncertainty was confirmed when they began asking directions. They were looking for a placed called Fresnes, just across the border in France, but they couldn't pronounce the word properly and drew only bewildered glances from the Belgians. Alex finally asked a Belgian girl the direction to Fresnes, pronouncing it correctly, and she pointed to a road to the left and told him it was about five kilometers, or three miles, away. The guards split up the column, and Alex and four others were motioned to follow the guard along the road to Fresnes.

They passed through the town of Condé, entering its narrow streets through an archway. The town was packed with French citizens and German soldiers. The column passed over a bridge that spanned a canal, and they were out in open country once more. All the while Alex was looking for a chance to escape. He figured he could simply drop out of the column without being seen, since his escort was growing careless, but he knew that in his present state of fatigue he wouldn't get far. Then again, he might be able to find a hiding place where he could rest up before starting for the Allied lines. After all, he still had his compass. When they stopped to rest he slipped next to Fleugel and told him his plans. Fleugel immediately begged to come along. "All right," Alex said, "be ready to leave as soon as we leave the village. Watch me. I'll say when." He was keyed up, his adrenaline flowing as he assessed their chances.

> Would we succeed? How long before they would discover that we had left the party? Would they start a search for us? As these questions flashed through my mind there was no room for consideration of how exhausted I was. I was keyed up for a supreme effort—a dash to freedom.
>
> Fleugel and I walked close to each other. Now and again we spoke in whispers, completing our final arrangements. We were now, I judged, about in the center of the village. We walked in silence. Everything was understood between us—we only awaited the moment.

The moment never arrived.

The guard had stopped to knock on a door. The door was promptly opened and the prisoners were ushered through a barbed-wire gate into an enclosure with a tall wire fence. There was a large building on the right and a row of low buildings on the left. Alex's heart sank. He was locked up again.

The guards marched him down an alley to a padlocked door. After unlocking the door, the guards motioned Alex into a small cell and locked the door behind him. The cell was twenty feet square with a nine-foot ceiling, and it contained a number of crude wooden beds. Alex stood blinking for a few moments until he realized that two of the beds were occupied.

The man in a top bunk stirred, rolled over, and sat up when he saw Alex. He recognized Alex's wings immediately. "American?" he said, "So am I." He was T. E. "Tilly" Tillinghast, of Westerly, Rhode Island, also a lieutenant in the air service.

Alex sat wearily and glanced at the other sleeping form. "Who is our friend in the corner?"

"He's a British tommy—the orderly for the officers in this cell. Gets our food from the cook and cleans out the room."

Alex was too tired for any more inquiries. He rolled over and fell asleep at once. It seemed like only seconds later that he was shaken awake by Rogers, the orderly, who held a steaming cup of coffee and a slice of sour bread. Alex added one of his biscuits to his meal and ate it quickly, much to the disgust of Tillinghast, who was so newly captured that he still couldn't stomach the food.

A commotion outside drew them to the window. A crowd of prisoners was scurrying past, most of them khaki-clad British, but here and there they saw a French uniform. There were easily two hundred men, all producing various kinds of bowls or dishes as they stood in rough formation waiting for coffee.

While they were watching, their cell door swung open, and a man in a British uniform entered the room. He informed him that although his uniform was British, he was an American, Lieutenant John Donaldson (whose father was a general, they later learned). Donaldson explained his British uniform with a story that excited Alex and resurfaced his yearning to escape. Donaldson had escaped from this very prison, only to be caught and returned. After his escape he had discarded his American uniform for civilian clothes he had managed to get, but he had made the mistake of walking through a small village where even a German soldier had recognized him as a stranger. When the soldier demanded his papers, Donaldson was trapped. When they brought him back, the Germans only had a British uniform to give him.

Since his escape the sentries had become doubly watchful, Donaldson told them. His own escape route had been over the roof at night. But later, another man took the same route and became entangled in the barbed wire. As he was disentangling himself from the wire in an attempt to surrender, the Germans shot him and left him hanging in the wire to bleed to death. Sentries now had instructions to shoot on sight anyone caught outside the quarters after dark.

In the daytime the prisoners were permitted to wander around the compound; only at night were the cells locked. Alex and his two companions went outside, where Alex began a close inspection of his surroundings. He was determined not to wait too long to make his move, knowing that he could be sent to Germany any day. Escaping from Germany would be nearly impossible, for he would have no civilian population to draw on for the help he was certain to find among the Belgians.

Alex saw a driveway that swept straight back from the main gates to a caretaker's cottage and stables, which obviously had been commandeered by the Huns and converted to a prison. The brick wall around the compound was about eight feet tall and topped by barbed wire. While he was looking around, the camp's commandant passed by on an inspection tour. "He was a big brute," Alex wrote,

> both as to height and girth, with an arrogant, haughty bearing. There were many tommys and French prisoners about who took no notice of him as he passed. Tillinghast and I had stopped walking and were standing to one side talking to each other, to watch him pass by. He saw us as he approached and recognized that we were officers. As he went by he turned toward us and saluted. We were so surprised that neither of us made a move to return his greeting. The tommys had not saluted him, why should we? He strode on, saying nothing, but we could see that he was inwardly raging.

Moments later the commandant sent for the two Americans, and he stormed at them through an interpreter for not saluting him. Alex replied that they weren't aware they were being saluted, which fooled no one, but apparently the interpreter smoothed things over. They had now come to the attention of the commandant, which was not an enviable position to be in.

The noon meal that day was sauerkraut soup that was so vinegary that not even Alex, who was now accustomed to prison fare, could eat it. He went back to Tillinghast and Donaldson to see what else he could learn. Shortly thereafter he was force to endure another unpleasant experience: a German intelligence officer sent for him and began to grill him in excellent English, particularly on the subject of whether new American squadrons were being formed. The officer was under the impression that Alex was from the same squadron as Tillinghast, a group that flew Sopwith Camels, and

Alex let him think whatever he wanted. Surprisingly, at the end of the interview, the German officer told him that he would be moved to another camp across the road, where he would be "more comfortable." Not long after, Alex was told to pack up and move. He said goodbye to his new friends and followed a guard down the long driveway to another camp.

He was led inside a cobblestone courtyard perhaps a hundred feet square. There was an L-shaped building that seemed to have once been a factory, a cookhouse on the left, an alleyway, and the main gate. In the center of the courtyard were benches on which a number of British prisoners sat, all wearing sergeant's or corporal's chevrons.

The prisoner nearest Alex offered to show him the sleeping quarters and also advised him that although this was a camp for noncommissioned officers, it also held a dozen Royal Air Force officers awaiting transportation to a prison in Germany. Some of the officers spotted Alex and came over to ply him with questions.

One of these officers was already a legend. Captain Halloran had lost both feet in the early days of the war, but he had them replaced with wooden feet that would allow him to work the pedals on a combat aircraft, and he soon got back into action. When he was captured he was a flight commander in his squadron. Alex had met him a month before, when Alex had been a dinner guest of two friends from another squadron. Now Halloran and Alex had a long talk in which Halloran told him that there were two other Americans in camp, but both were in solitary confinement—they had attempted to escape and were caught. They were allowed to come into the courtyard, where as a relief from their bread-and-water diet they could sneak other food from friends. One of the Americans was Donaldson, the other was a Lieutenant Mandell. Just thinking of escape made the day drag on monotonously. Alex joined the other prisoners as they brewed tea, then he found himself a space near one of the few windows and threw down his mattress.

The next day Alex had time for only a few words with Donaldson in the courtyard. That night his sleep was restless, and when he went outside he could get only as far as the bottom of the stairs before the sentry turned him back. Escape. Escape. It was what he lived for now.

At noon the next day he got what he considered his first real break: Tillinghast was moved over into the camp, and later in the day Alex, Tillinghast, and Donaldson were able to meet and talk. The camp was rife with rumors; it seemed that since there were now eighteen or twenty officers in the camp it was time to move them on to Germany. Donaldson suggested that the three of them ask Mandell to join them, as Mandell had been chatting with the guard in German, Donaldson said, and he and the guard had become quite friendly. Perhaps if Mandell were among the escapees the guard would not stop them. Alex knew time was becoming critical, for they could be moved at any time. They went to meet Mandell immediately:

> The three of us proceeded across the yard into the guard-room. Mandell rose to greet us. We all sat down, two on the floor and two on the bed. I squatted on the floor near the one little window that overlooked the main gates and the courtyard. Tillinghast and I were, of course, most interested in the escape that our new friends had recently made. We plied them with question after question until finally we had the whole story. Why not escape again?
>
> The afternoon gradually wore away. The campfires were lit. I was standing near one of them, helping to get dinner, when I turned to find Mandell at my shoulder. They would be off that night, he told me quietly, so that none of the others heard. Then he went on saying something. Would I like to go along with them? That was it; they wanted me to join the party and escape with them.

It was decided. There would be five in the party: Alex, Donaldson, Tillinghast, Mandell, and the English corporal, Rogers. "The more the merrier," Mandell said cheerily. Alex was ecstatic. *At last*, he thought.

CHAPTER 8

The islands that Alex loved were a long way from the European war, but the war touched the people of Hawai'i in ways that Alex—now gearing up for a daring escape attempt—could not imagine. For his parents and his sister, Ruth, the war was very real, and for them it was embodied in that young boy who was so suddenly a man and so desperately in peril. But for others the war seemed distant and somewhat unreal. This soon changed, bringing near hysteria to Honolulu.

It began with a ship. Before the United States entered the war Hawai'i was a neutral port that offered a safe harbor to ships of any nation. Many ships took advantage of this neutrality, nosing into Honolulu Harbor to wait and watch the conduct of the war. One such ship was a German gunboat, the *Geier,* commanded by Captain Grasshof. During the time that the ship was in port, the U.S. and Germany broke off diplomatic relations, and the Germans began unrestricted submarine warfare. Even after these events the *Geier* remained, and the people of Honolulu became concerned. The German ship, in fact, had overstayed its allotted time in port. The ship was seized by the U.S. government (and eventually joined the American Navy), and the Captain's journal was confiscated. In his journal the captain mentioned George Rodiek, who was first vice president and ranking officer of one of Hawai'i's largest firms—H. Hackfeld and Company—and president of the influential Hawai'i Sugar Planters Association. Heinrich Schroeder, a Hackfeld employee and former secretary to the German consul, was also mentioned.

There was an uproar. If the head of one of Hawai'i's businesses might have aided the enemy, who else could be involved? Rodiek was fined ten thousand dollars and lost his U.S. citizenship (it was returned four years later by President Wilson). Schroeder was also fined, although his fine was only one thousand dollars. The superintendent of Queen's Hospital was accused of pro-German sentiments, and although the accusation was never proved, he resigned in the furor. A newspaper demanded to know if the manager of a large department store was pro-German.

Public school teachers had to sign a loyalty oath, and German-language courses were dropped from the University of Hawai'i and were not reinstated until 1927. Public schools also dropped all German-language courses. Hawaiians with German-sounding names suffered undeserved persecution, and many German families packed up and left the islands. A Vigilance Corps was formed to keep an eye on "hostile influences." There was talk of interning some German families.

At the start of 1918 there were about two hundred islanders overseas, many of whom were members of the armed forces, like Alex, and there were others who were ambulance drivers and nurses. Hawai'i residents bought war bonds, and not everyone succumbed to the incipient hysteria brought on by the war. Still, changes came because of the war. H. Hackfeld and Company had forty thousand shares of stock outstanding, with more than twenty-seven thousand shares owned by German citizens. The U.S. government seized the Germans' stock under the Trading with the Enemy Act and then sold it, mostly to island businessmen. H. Hackfeld and Company, now under new ownership, was renamed American Factors. Hackfeld's department store, B. F. Ehlers and Company, was renamed Liberty House. A Honolulu newspaper invited people to a change-of-name ceremony in which, trumpeted a headline, "All Traces of Teutonism Within and Without Will Be Removed."

To the degree it was possible, Hawai'i mobilized. At 'Iolani Palace, Governor Charles J. McCarthy drew the first order number for the draft. A Hawaiian naval militia was formed, as were the Japanese War Savings Stamp Committee and the Boys Working Reserve Group. The Yeomanettes donned sailor's uniforms and went to work. Training was intensified at Schofield Barracks, and at the Makiki Fire Station firemen not answering a fire call spent their time knitting for the war effort.

The planning was finished, for better or for worse. Now was the time for action, and Alex knew what his options were—to make a successful escape, to be caught and returned to prison camp to face punishment, or to become entangled in the barbed wire and shot, left to see his life running out in little rivulets of blood.

He dressed in all the clothing he had, donning two of the Red Cross flannel shirts with his khaki shirt over them, and found that he was barely able to button his jacket. He loaded his pockets with small articles that he thought might somehow be useful and slipped his compass into his pants pocket. He looked at his wristwatch; it was six o'clock on an evening that seemed to be holding darkness in check. It was too light, Alex thought. But there were still men walking around in the courtyard, and this was an advantage. Donaldson, Alex, and Tillinghast walked through the courtyard and into the guard room, through which they had to pass to get to the room from which they would escape.

The guard room already was lighted by lamps, and two Germans were playing checkers at a table, hardly glancing up as the prisoners entered. Donaldson led the little party across the room and up a flight of stairs, whistling. Alex could have done without the whistling. Alex remembered the time that followed well:

> Once upstairs we all sat down to wait for darkness. We maintained a strict silence for a long time. Our object was to avoid reminding the Huns below of the presence of Tillinghast and myself. We hoped that in the interest of their game they would not give us a second

thought. We waited while the twilight grew fainter and the shadows deeper. I glanced at my wristwatch. Its luminous dial showed eight o'clock. A moment later a tinny-sounding piano tinkled out a lively tune in the still night. The Huns who lived there were celebrating.

"We'll start about ten," Mandell whispered. "That ought to give the Huns next door a chance to get to bed. Rogers knows we're coming; he'll have everything ready." After that none of us spoke for ages it seemed. I could feel my heart pump faster at the thought of the approaching moment. Would me make it?

Downstairs the Germans pushed the checkerboard aside and scraped their chairs as they got up from the game. The prisoners held their breath, for this was the crucial moment. Would the guards come upstairs and discover them, or would they wander off to bed? The moments seemed to last forever, and all eyes were on the door at the bottom of the stairs. The door never opened.

"Get ready to move." Alex heard the order loud and clear.

"I had been sitting on my flying suit. Now I stood up cautiously, throwing the suit over my arm. I reached to my hip-pocket to draw forth my civilian cap and put it on. I slung a bag of biscuits over my shoulder."

Mandell took the lead since he was the expert at removing the locks. He got the first door open easily, and Tillinghast, Alex, and Donaldson followed him out. The second door was already open, and Rogers awaited them there. Inside the room, Alex looked up and saw a hole in the roof two feet above his head. The plan was to go through the hole one at a time, the first man watching for the second and so on, until they were all safely on the roof; then they would climb down from the roof and drop into the courtyard one by one. This time Rogers led the way; Alex was fourth in the procession, with Donaldson bringing up the rear.

Rogers got onto the roof easily enough, then froze. For ten long minutes he held his position, not daring to move, while the others waited in apprehension. Finally, Rogers hissed, "Come on," and they heard the rattle of tiles as he scampered across the roof.

They went up and through the roof without too much difficulty, and a moment later Alex was following Tillinghast down from the roof and into the courtyard. They moved across the yard and past a lighted window, where they saw movement inside the room. Not all the Huns were in bed. They reached a portion of the wall where a mound of dirt had been piled up to help them over. Alex never knew who did this or when it was done, he just climbed up the mound onto and over the wall.

To our left was the main street of the village, solidly lined with houses. To our right, parallel with the street, was the canal that flowed past the back door of the prison camp. We turned now to the right, making for the canal.

There we turned left and followed a footpath that skirted it. Our progress was slow because of numerous fences, some of them board, others wire and still others picket fences, that ran down to the very water's edge. We must either climb over them or, when it was possible, swing round the end that usually projected out over the water

We had been out of prison about an hour and were still within a quarter of a mile of the camp, when the moon came up over distant houses and trees. It shone directly down the canal. It was beautiful, but it was so disconcertingly bright. It seemed light as day.

Crouching and weaving through shadows, the men kept moving until they came to a large, brightly lit building. It was a factory that hummed with activity day and night. They were passing the factory when a German voice called, "Halt!" The voice came from the direction of the factory. Alex and Donaldson, without hesitation, shouted back in unison, "Was ist?"

"There was a dead silence after that," Alex recalled. "Ostrich-like I attempted to bury my head between my shoulders, waiting for that ping sound past my ear that would announce the opening of hostilities. But nothing happened."

The men stumbled on ahead. It was past midnight and they were making good progress, but they were growing weary and hungry. A wagon rattled past them on the road, and they hid in a nearby field. As they came up to a river they suddenly knew exactly where they were, and it was only four or five miles from Fresnes. Suddenly there were more wagons, and once again they hid in the brush.

They spent the next hours slipping past houses and avoiding lighted areas, where there were sure to be sentries. They followed the edge of the woods, ready to flee at any moment. As they passed a barn they were startled

CHAPTER 9

by the deep-throated barking of a dog, and the sound followed them long after they were clear of the barn. They turned north and crept along, and to their dismay they aroused another dog, which led to a whole chorus of barking dogs. Someone in a nearby house threw open a window, and a challenge was issued to the night. Other windows opened, and it seemed the entire village had taken up the cry. A bullet whizzed past them as they headed for the nearby trees. It was becoming clear that they needed a place to hide. They stopped long enough to drink water from a stream.

Rogers and Mandell decided to go on a foraging expedition, and they crept up to the nearest house to scrounge for food, while Alex, Tillinghast, and Donaldson were left to make camp in a small grove of trees. Alex remembered working feverishly to construct some sort of hidden shelter, but with the coming of daylight the little shelter looked pitifully insecure. The small trees they bent to form a rough canopy seemed thin, and the whole aspect of the shelter was one of decided vulnerability.

Daylight revealed that they were on the edge of a beet field, so Alex crept out and pulled a few beets to nibble on. While they were nibbling, they looked up to see Mandell and Rogers returning. The men in the shelter were thunderstruck to see their friends coming toward them with armloads of bread and potatoes—and a bright blue coffeepot! Rogers explained that he'd simply walked up to the door of a nearby farmhouse and begged for food.

Now the escapees discussed the advisability of doing this at another farmhouse on the other side of the fields. Their horizons were expanding—now it wasn't only food they craved, but also a map and civilian clothing.

It was Rogers who made the bold move; he confidently approached a French farmer in a nearby field while the others remained in the grove of trees. After a lengthy conversation he was back, beaming. The farmer was going to help them. The farmer and his wife disappeared for a time, then they reappeared, walking toward the trees, each carrying a large bundle. Inside the circle of trees, the farmer and his wife opened the bags and produced more food—coffee, bread, and potatoes—and an assortment of civilian clothing. They also brought a warning: Germans patrolled the area along a path by the stream just outside the woods. In addition, there was a German artillery-training school nearby.

The farmer invited the escapees to visit his home before they continued their journey, and they accepted happily. But first they had to get around the German patrol. It turned out to be a solitary Hun soldier who walked rather woodenly, certainly not very alertly, along the path. He passed within twenty yards of the men hidden in the trees and proceeded on down the path. Alex, now wearing a fur overcoat and a civilian cap, moved quickly with the others in a dash for the farmer's house.

In the kitchen of the modest home they found the farmer's family and the family of his son, which made for pleasantly crowded conditions. Nevertheless, places were cleared for the five escapees, who found themselves staring in wonder at great bowls of soup and steaming potatoes. Then their host brought out a map; they were in a small village on the French-Belgian border, only five miles from the prison—although they had covered at least twenty miles in their wanderings. Brussels lay some forty miles to the northeast. Unwilling to let go of the idea of stealing a German airplane, the escapees asked if there were any German airfields nearby. They were told that there was one just beyond the Tournai-Ath canal and the main railway line.

By order of his Imperial Majesty, the Kaiser, no Belgian was allowed on the streets of his own country after ten o'clock at night. Alex and his friends left the hospitality of the farmer and his family and began to walk boldly, in their civilian clothes, through the streets of the village well before the curfew. They passed through unchallenged and got into the countryside, and by nine o'clock they were in a second village, then they reached the canal. The bridge over the canal was deserted; beyond it they could see the railway not more than a hundred yards away.

A sentry suddenly appeared with a lantern to take up his post in a gatebox. Moving off to the right, the escapees found themselves passing a building where they heard German voices. Alex felt his heart pounding with the crunch of their shoes on the gravel, surely loud enough to be heard by the Germans. Suddenly a steady rain came, creating a patter on the roof of the building, and the five men breathed a sigh of relief as they hastened away.

Alex was now using the compass he had managed to keep, holding them to a generally northern direction. At two in the morning he glanced at the compass then looked up to see a large farmhouse in their path. Buoyed by their recent successes, they pushed Rogers forward to knock on the door to ask the occupants for shelter. Rogers reluctantly beat on the door of the farmhouse, conscious of the hour and of the blackness of the night.

An hour later the five escapees were seated in front of a roaring fire in the farmer's living room, while in the kitchen the lady of the house was making coffee and slicing bread. Their hospitality was generous, but the farmer was startled when Rogers asked if they could hide out in his house for a day. It was too dangerous, he said, and he advised them to go another mile down the road—leaving before daybreak—and ask the farmer in a large house there if they could stay in his barn.

They found the second farmhouse easily enough, and by now they had no hesitation in knocking on the door and asking for help. The owner agreed to hide them in the basement of a large smokestack on a knoll across the road from his house. They proceeded through a tunnel, past an unused oven, and into a room with a great pile of straw on the floor. The men immediately fell into a deep sleep.

They were awakened by a strange voice and a beam of light. It was an electric torch held by a man who introduced himself as the miller of the village of Quevaucamps. The escapees pulled out their map and decided they must have traveled west of the airdrome they were seeking. They decided to press on to Brussels, which meant they would have to branch off to the northeast, keeping well to the south of the town of Ath, where there was a large German force.

Greatly refreshed, they set off again, walking from seven at night until three in the morning, resting ten minutes of every hour. Each time they approached a village they detoured around it. Alex, scouting some fifty yards ahead of the party, had a close call when he was starting across a road. Hearing a footstep, he ducked back into the shrubbery alongside the road and watched as a German soldier passed. Most of the time the men held to the wagon roads, crossing streams occasionally and once tramping with difficulty through a large field of turnips. Now and then they passed through a darkened village. At about two o'clock one morning they crossed the Ath-Péruwelz railroad and shortly afterward the main canal, and they felt a sense of accomplishment.

Early in the morning, in the village of Maffle, a few miles southeast of Ath, they knocked on the door of a Belgian farmer; when he opened the door all five heads tilted upward to stare at a huge man whose face was both kind and strong. He gathered them in at once, built a fire to warm them, then led them through his house out to a cottage where there were beds. Beds! Even crowded three in a double bed and two in a single, they slept like logs, interrupted only when the giant farmer brought them soup, potatoes, and bread. He also gave them his only suit, which was a fine-looking brown suit. Mandell was the only one who could wear it, and even on him it was still too large, but at least now only three of the five escapees were still in uniform. When they got ready to leave that evening, the farmer advised them to stay on the south side of the Ath-Enghien road, and his wife presented them with a huge, round loaf of bread and some potatoes.

Then Alex and the others got a shock. Instead of leading them out into the countryside again, the giant farmer took them straight to an inn and led them boldly inside, where he ordered beer for all. Alex looked around; there were several villagers in the room. But the huge farmer was expansive, ordering beer and telling the villagers that these were escaped Allies, fleeing the Huns. The villagers crowded around, talking excitedly about the escape and offering advice. In time the escapees were able to get away, and they melted gratefully into the darkness. A moment later they discovered that the huge farmer was with them still, for he collected them on a riverbank, cupped his hands, and called for the ferry, then he entrusted them to the care of a ferryman who appeared with his boat and took them across the river.

CHAPTER 9

On they trekked, angling for the border of Belgium and Holland. Guided by Alex's precious compass and often knocking on doors to ask for food and shelter, during the month of October 1918 they made their way across occupied Belgium. Alex later recalled that "many a time during our escape, wet, cold and exhausted, we reached the point where we had utterly no regard for our safety. Then it was comfort first, with a reckless disregard for consequences."

George Rogers had a friend named Voghel who lived on the outskirts of Brussels, and he had been concocting a plan to get to Voghel, who lived on the rue Saint Augustin, to seek help crossing the border. That crossing was viewed, quite rightly, as the most dangerous part of the escape. Taking Mandell with him, Rogers went off to seek his friend. They never came back.

A long time afterwards, Alex learned that Mandell and Rogers had been caught on the border and taken back into custody by German troops. That day seemed endless to Alex, Donaldson, and Tillinghast as they waited for their friends to reappear and began to realize that they were not likely to return. That afternoon, lying up in the loft of a farmer's house, Alex raised the subject of an airdrome with the Belgian, who confirmed that there was an air base nearby and agreed to lead them there in the evening. True to his word, he arrived in the darkness and showed them the road that lead to the airdrome.

But now the hour was late, and the men decided to hide for another night before attempting to reconnoiter the base. Confidently, Alex knocked on a farmhouse door, but in a hurried conversation he ran into a rare refusal of help. "Why won't you help us?" Alex asked the farmer. "Les Allemands," the farmer replied, shrugging, explaining that the Germans operated a factory just across the road, and by dawn there would be thousands of them turning out to work.

The three escapees moved out fast, slipping through the countryside and into the outskirts of a town. At one point they paused wearily below a street sign then gazed at it in wonder: the rue Saint Augustin. Hoping for assistance, they went down the block and soon found Voghel's house, number twenty-four. Alex knocked, then called out softly in the darkness. After a time a woman's voice came back to him, with a hint of mistrust in it. No, she said, Voghel wasn't home; he was in prison.

The men pushed on with a growing feeling of desperation. Daylight was coming, they were in an urban area with few readily apparent hiding places, and there were Germans about. In fact, there was a man coming in their direction now, and with a burst of energy the three men turned and went over the wall they had been walking beside.

It was a fortuitous move. They found themselves on a large estate with a grove of trees nearby—an excellent, if wet and cold, hiding place. Beyond it they could see the owner's house, to one side of which was what they decided was a summerhouse. It had a chimney, which meant it had a stove or fireplace, which meant getting warm and dry. Not hesitating, they went into the house to find that there was, indeed, a stove and enough wood for a fire. Soon they were thawing in front of the stove, a delicious moment that ended abruptly when the door was flung open— there stood a man with a ferocious mustache and an equally dangerous-looking axe. "Oh, such a time as I had with that gardener before finally winning him over to be friendly," Alex would recall. "I simply told him all I could about us, the other boys backing me up by exhibiting their flying equipment. Finally we convinced him of our integrity. He apologized for having been so hostile at first, explaining that the city was full of German deserters. He had taken us for Huns." But, the gardener noted, he had to get permission from Madame in the chateau for the three to remain. He would go talk to her, he said, and come back.

Instead, a slim figure clad in a white skirt and a yellow sweater-jacket approached the summer house next, a lovely girl speaking perfect English who was the daughter of the Madame. The men, all quite awestruck by this apparition, found their tongues and poured out their story.

60   CHAPTER 10

The girl promised to convince her mother to let them stay. She disappeared back up the winding path.

Soon she was back, this time accompanied by her mother and sister, who were trailed by a servant carrying a huge basket of beer, food, and books. Madame hoped they would be comfortable. "Three of the luckiest prisoners of war that ever breathed," Alex noted.

After a luncheon in which the escapees had meat for the first time in a long time and white bread for the first time since their capture, the three were visited again by the two sisters. It would be best to move, the sisters said, since their father, who was away in town at the moment, might disapprove if he found them here. The sisters suggested that the three move to the house of the younger daughter, which was on the grounds of the estate but several hundred yards from the main house.

In minutes they found themselves in a large upstairs bedroom of the younger daughter's home. There they had a hot bath, a shave, and a chance to wash their clothes and hang them up to dry. After a nap they joined their hostess for tea, marveling at the snowy white tablecloths, the real sugar for tea, and the delicious bread. Their hostess was Madame Verhaeghe. The daughter whose home they were in was Madame Van den Corput. Both daughters were wives of Belgian army officers who had slipped across the border into Holland to hook up with Allied forces and take part in the war.

Alex, ever persistent, brought up the subject of the airdrome, and was immediately disappointed. It wasn't an air base, the sisters told him, it was a factory for manufacturing engines.

The day continued to be something of a fairy tale: at seven o'clock dinner appeared and almost overwhelmed the three men. They were served soup, roast beef, potatoes, vegetables, pudding, coffee, and wine. Nothing, they thought, could top this. But then as the men got ready to leave, the two sisters brought out an array of men's clothing, enough civilian clothing to completely hide their uniforms. They also produced two large-scale Belgian Touring Club maps, detailed and easy to read, and another round of food to take with them—bread, meat, potatoes, and sugar. Alex vowed that one day, after the war, he'd come back and thank these benefactors for their unselfish help.

As they said goodbye, Madame's chauffeur, a young man, asked permission to guide them through the streets of Brussels and get them on the road where, ultimately, they would be near the border of Holland.

Soon they were on the Chaussée de Gand, the road to Ghent, and eventually they came to the Gare de l'Ouest and crossed under the railroad bridge. The chauffeur turned back.

While they were resting on the curbing, the three men were suddenly approached by a Belgian policeman, who demanded to know what they were doing there and to see the contents of their knapsacks. Alex decided that honesty was the best policy, and he told him their story, unable to resist adding that he still wanted to steal an airplane and fly it home. The policeman thought it was a great story, and he wished them luck and left them.

He soon came back, this time with a fellow policeman. The officers warned that there were many, many Germans about, and suggested they accompany the policemen back to their apartment in the rue des Quatre Vents. Alex felt a small chill as they walked openly through the streets, passing German soldiers, but the soldiers never gave them a second glance.

The next day, emboldened by their success and feeling now that their civilian clothing was as effective as a suit of armor, the three ventured into the street and stopped for a meal. Alex grew so confident as to ask for a barber shop, and he was directed to a shop "run by a loyal Belgian. He won't give you away," he was told.

Tillinghast was in the barber's chair and Alex and Donaldson were waiting when a German officer came in for a shave. There was a collective holding of breath. The barber, with great presence of mind, abandoned Tillinghast and attended the German, who was mollified by the attention. When his shave was completed, the officer left the barber shop without so much as a glance at the three escapees.

Meanwhile, Alex was thinking about Rogers and Mandell. He didn't want to just forget about them, so he decided to go back to the rue Saint Augustin 24, in spite of all the risks that such a journey entailed, to see if he could learn more. In a little wine shop where Tillinghast and Donaldson were to wait for him, Alex got instructions on how to take a bus to his destination. While he was waiting for the bus, he noticed that almost every bus that came by disgorged large numbers of Huns, and he finally decided to walk. It was noon before he reached the door he had knocked on at four o'clock the morning before.

The same woman appeared, but this time she was more amiable. Yes, she told Alex, Voghel was in prison until next February, and yes, two men had appeared the day before Alex's first visit. They had asked her to shelter them, but she didn't dare, so they left. She gave Alex bread and a bowl of soup for lunch, and told him how to have the correct fare for the bus going back so he wouldn't have to talk to the conductor. Alex rode back to the wine shop standing on the back platform with a German soldier who, fortunately, was too haughty to talk to him.

In a hasty conference at the wine shop, the three men decided that Rogers and Mandell had either gotten over the border on their own or been recaptured. They also decided that they would humor Alex, who had heard of a nearby airdrome, by investigating the possibility of stealing an airplane. They got back on a bus, standing on a back platform together, and got off at the end of the line, which was, indeed, a German air base.

The air base consisted of a huge hangar in the center of the field that had probably, Alex thought, once been a hangar for large observation balloons. It was surrounded by a high fence, and even worse, the hangars were closed and locked and the doors looked impenetrable. Nearby there was an inn, where a sympathetic woman listened to their questions but gave them discouraging answers. Yes, she said, she thought there were quite a few Hun sentries about the field at night. Before she could continue, some Germans came in, and the men casually but quickly slipped out of the inn.

Alex was more than a little annoyed. Why couldn't the Germans be as casual about their base security as his own people were? He might have been able to make off with one of the clumsy two-seaters he'd seen flying around the field.

En route back to the bus, the three got their worst fright in days. Some ten German flying officers stood in their path, obviously waiting for transportation. There was no choice but to brazen it out. But as Tillinghast and Donaldson walked by the soldiers, the Germans decided to have some fun—they edged over and nudged the two men off the road. The Huns laughed uproariously as Tillinghast and Donaldson went flying to the side of the road. Alex, his heart in his mouth, walked steadily onward, unmolested. The three escapees regrouped and caught the bus back to the friendly wine shop.

Alex finally gave up the idea of flying home. They would have to go the hard, traditional way through the electric fences and into Holland, a venture that held more than one kind of hazard. Not only were the fences electrified, but there were numerous sentry boxes with sentries experienced in turning back would-be escapees.

The men decided to catch a small two-car train that would speed things along. With one of their host policemen carrying their knapsack, they walked through the streets to the train station and were soon aboard, occupying the front platform of the trailer to the train. Donaldson stowed the knapsack at his feet, and the three escapees remained silent in the presence of several German soldiers.

The train pulled out. "It was," Alex said later, "the most nerve-racking ride I have ever taken." Alex's overcoat slipped down, and a fellow passenger began eyeing the flight suit Alex still wore underneath. Alex hastily pulled his coat up again. He felt his heart pounding as he looked over to see that a German officer had boarded the train, escorting a Red Cross nurse, and was standing not two feet away from Donaldson. Suddenly Donaldson seemed to be shrinking—his head moved down and suddenly disappeared. Horrified, Alex caught a glimpse of Donaldson on the floor of the train, head and shoulders hanging down as he reached for the knapsack that slid from his feet. As the train jerked forward, Donaldson made a final, desperate grab for the knapsack, and one foot came back and kicked a fellow passenger—the German officer. Alex held his breath.

"Had it not been for the nurse," Alex said, "the Hun probably would have been dangerously ugly . . . as it was he contented himself with a good, round cursing, which did none of us any harm. We were much relieved when a few stations later the Boche and his lady left the car."

The train continued to disgorge passengers at the stations, and the passengers thinned out until only the escapees and five or six Germans were still aboard. Finally, it was time for them to leave the train. They were now on a road heading northeast again, once more trudging in the darkness—three desperate men on the final and most dangerous leg of their journey.

For Alex and his companions, trekking in silence and in darkness toward a frontier that held both hope and hazard, the war was immediate and personal, and at the time they had no realization of the magnitude of what was to be the war to end all wars. Statistics had not yet been compiled, but when they were, they reflected the dedication, commitment, and desperation of the people who fought a war that took place on three continents and was as brutal and deadly as any war that had come before it.

Dictators had made Europe and the Middle East the testing ground of their rivalries many times in the past. Now the old rivalries had surfaced, and they erupted in extreme violence. Beginning with Austria-Hungary's attack on Serbia on July 29, 1914, and Germany's swift invasion of Belgium on August 4, the war escalated to involve not only Europeans, but also Turkey and Arabia, various Middle Eastern tribes, and the United States.

In the first three weeks of the war nearly a million men were lost to death, wounds, or capture. When the war deteriorated into trench warfare it became a nightmare of cold, filth, stench, boredom, and danger. It was an era of megacasualties. In four months at the Somme, the British suffered 410,000 casualties, the French 195,000, and the Germans 500,000. Near Ypres, Belgium, on April 22, 1915, the Germans ushered in a terrifying new aspect of the war when they released chlorine gas, bringing terror and death.

In July 1917 an allied offensive was launched near Ypres to take the 150-foot-high Passchendaele Ridge. It took four months and three hundred thousand British casualties to take the ridge. In the war at sea, German U-boats in the first four months of 1917 were sinking an average of ten ships a day. As the war continued there were concomitant hardships at home.

By war's end some 4.8 million Americans had served in the armed forces. Battle names were entered into folklore—Belleau Woods, the Hindenburg Line, the Marne. There were heroes, some of whom entered into America's folklore. A conscientious objector from Tennessee, private Alvin C. York, overcame his feelings in a rush of patriotism and went on to win the Medal of Honor.

Historians estimate that some sixty-five million men were involved in World War I and that at least ten million of them died in combat and twice that many were wounded. As many as four million civilians also died. The map of Europe was changed dramatically, only to change again in a few short years with the advent of World War II.

World War I began less than a dozen years after the Wright brothers' historic flight at Kitty Hawk, North Carolina. Airplanes added a new dimension to war, and their evolution kept pace with industrial innovations in other fields. The pilots, no matter how dashing and gallant their lives appeared, died in horrific numbers: of the 150,000 or so airmen in the war, about one-third of them—some 50,000 young men—were killed in action.

The three escapees now moving across northern Belgium had no way of knowing it at the time, but they were among the lucky ones. The average life span of a pilot flying combat patrols at the front was only three weeks.

CHAPTER 11

Alex awoke abruptly to an elbow digging into his ribs. "They're coming after us," came a whisper, and he looked up to see a group of Belgian men advancing on the patch of woods where the three airmen had been hiding. Now in the Flemish-speaking north of Belgium, the escapees were finding Alex's French less useful and the people less cordial; they had been turned away from a couple of farmhouses. Tensions were running high.

"The leader of the group," Alex remembered,

> was a tall, raw-boned individual with a long, iron-gray beard. He had a sort of meat cleaver in his determined grasp and there was a dangerous look in his eye . . . they came up and surrounded us. The leader approached within a few yards. In threatening tones he wanted to know what we were doing here.
>
> At first he would not admit that he knew French, but I could see that he understood something of what I said, so I just fired away at him with a complete history of us. I won him over at last, and the change in his manner was miraculous From a hostile, menacing attitude he changed to one of most cordial friendship. He explained that they had taken us for Hun deserters.

Twice during the day the leader showed up with food, and in time the three escapees moved on.

At one farm the men met a young girl fluent in French who provided the escapees with food and a bed. The girl also wrote them a note in

Flemish that they could show to others along the way, explaining who they were and what they were trying to do.

As luck would have it, the next person they appealed to for help was a woman who spoke good English. She explained that her husband was a British jockey who was still in Belgium, evading Germans by passing as a Belgian in spite of his lack of a passport. A second Englishman, also a jockey, turned up at her home and later led the escapees to the home of still another Englishman and ultimately to the home of François Timmerman, chairman of the national committee charged with distributing food received from America. He distributed food freely to the three escapees, who had plenty to eat and a good night's sleep at Timmerman's home before starting out again.

At four o'clock the next afternoon they reached the village of Ramsel. Here the note written in Flemish came in handy, and they were able to rest in the loft of a farmhouse. In the middle of the afternoon a young boy woke them and said they were wanted downstairs. With some trepidation they descended to the main room of the farmhouse. Waiting for them was a black-robed priest, who spoke French. Alex explained who they were and what they were attempting to do. The priest warned them of the border hazards, then showed them a map, pointing out the Abbaye Tongerloo some twelve kilometers to the northeast, and suggesting that the escapees go there and tell the priests he had sent them.

By nine o'clock that evening they had reached the abbey, where they were welcomed by a Frenchwoman and her husband, then joined by another couple. Alex quickly learned that there were some seventy or eighty exiles from the war living under the protection of the abbey. The Father Superior and another priest, Father Dockx, appeared, and it turned out that Father Dockx spoke excellent English. The three Americans were welcomed to the abbey, given a satisfying meal, and put to bed for the night.

The next day Father Dockx conferred with the three escapees, showing them a large-scale map of the area between the abbey and the frontier. It was helpful but sobering, for the Germans were numerous, the border was well guarded, and the fences were electrified. Nevertheless, the men set off again, keeping ever to the northeast.

They passed through Zammel and stopped at the church in Rauw, where the priest fed them and sent them on. In a moment that was pure serendipity, they stopped at a bicycle repair shop and began questioning the middle-aged man about directions. In the middle of Alex's French, the man suddenly asked, "Do you speak English?"

Alex remembered, "A thunderclap could hardly have taken us more by surprise." The man was Gus Hus, who had spent years in America and Canada as a bricklayer. While they were talking, Hus suddenly jumped up and ran to the window, hailing a man who was driving by. Soon he brought a man who resembled him into the room. "This is my brother, Jan Hus," he said. The brothers got into a long discussion, the result being the decision that Jan would search the surrounding villages for a guide to lead the escapees to the border.

The men now had nothing to do but wait. They were well fed, but at one point they had to sleep outdoors in a thicket. The Hus brothers were scurrying about the countryside, looking for a suitable guide.

Jan Hus invited the escapees to his home, where he hoped they would be more comfortable. As they rode in his pony cart, they passed a number of Belgians who gave Jan a signal that all was clear. Alex surmised that the entire countryside knew of their presence. He hoped the Huns did not, and was relieved when they passed a station platform filled with German soldiers, none of whom gave them a second glance.

At Jan Hus's home the three men were warm, dry, and secure—or so they thought. One Tuesday morning two German soldiers knocked on the door and demanded to see Jan Hus. Alex recalled that incident clearly:

> We were quickly hustled out through the back door and down through a cellar window into a dark, musty, dungeon-like place to wait while Jan received his callers. At the end of 15 minutes he came down to get us, the Germans having departed. They would be back presently, however. These two had been making arrangements to billet 20 or more of them with Jan for the night. It seemed that some 200 would be entering the town at nightfall. After much discussion between Jan and his friends, he told us he would be willing to take a chance if we would. We could stay in this room with the doors and windows locked. Most of the Huns would be quartered in the stable. Three of the officers would, however, occupy a room on the second floor.
>
> It was ten o'clock when Jan came to report that all his Huns were safely tucked away. Taking our shoes off, we tiptoed up the creaking stairs. Jan had already removed the outside knobs from our doors so that once inside with the doors closed, they could not easily be opened from without.

The Germans spent the night and the next day in Jan's home, never suspecting that three escaped Americans were hiding in the same place. The following day the Germans left, and the escapees—and Jan Hus—breathed easier.

One Saturday afternoon the three airmen got the word they had been waiting for—the guide had been found! That afternoon the guide showed up—a tall, slim, fair-haired man of perhaps thirty. By four o'clock that afternoon Jan's friends came in to say goodbye. Monday morning came, and with it came presents of clothing from Jan. Now they were really going, and two other men, named Georges and Sew, were going with them. With the guide would be two assistants. It was a sizeable party.

The first step was to get to the house where the guide lived, which entailed crossing a bridge near a factory, a dangerously exposed crossing. Safely across, they reached the guide's home, where his mother prepared coffee. Alex learned that three Frenchmen would be joining them as well, in a group that was growing larger all the time. Still, he remained optimistic.

The three Frenchmen soon arrived. It was decided that the crossing would be attempted at three in the morning, and everyone was advised to get some sleep. Alex huddled in a corner and found it hard to fall asleep. He spent most of the night watching the young guide get ready for the crossing.

There came a sobering moment: one by one the guide searched them all for concealed weapons, explaining that he had no intention of being shot in the back by any Hun spy who might have infiltrated the group. Then he advised them that at the crossing, everybody was to go through with it, that he would not hesitate to shoot anybody who turned back once they were on the way.

The guide also collected his fees. Georges and Sew were required to pay the guide five hundred francs each; the Americans and the three Frenchmen, being soldiers, were exempted.

At three o'clock they pushed off. Recent rains had made such bogs that the guide, cursing, was forced to lead them on detours. They stopped for breakfast in a stand of trees then trekked across some main roads—the Lille St. Hubert–Petit Brogel Road and the Petit Brogel–Weert Highway. Alex was cheered to think of Weert—it was in Holland. During the rest stop the guide explained the crossing and the greatest hazard: between the fences were trenches filled with water, and a misstep into any one of them would make a splash that would give them away.

When they resumed the trek, Alex began to feel his exhaustion. In the past twenty-four hours he had slept only about four hours, and he had eaten only three sandwiches. But he also felt excitement knowing that the weeks of hiding and walking, of fear in the presence of German troops, of hunger and cold, were coming to an end.

They moved off the main road and onto a narrow road that pointed like an arrow to the northeast. The guide halted them at the edge of a tree line, went into the trees, and emerged with a pair of rubber hip boots he had dug up from the place they had been cached. He put on the boots, then Alex saw that he also had heavy rubber gauntlets and a pair of wire clippers. The guide was careful to wipe all traces of moisture from the rubber handles of the clippers. The party moved forward in strict silence.

The moon, Alex recalled, was merciless in its brilliance, but then they entered a light fog. Moving quickly but quietly, they came to the first water ditch. They went through it on hands and knees and came to the second, then there were ditches every five yards. Alarmingly, someone's foot dragged and splashed in the water.

There was a shout that froze them all. An answering shout came from a hundred yards away, and Alex breathed a sigh of relief; it was only the sentries calling to each other. The escapees were now close enough to the sentries to hear them when they coughed.

They crawled through the last fifty yards of a clearing, stopping for ten to fifteen minutes at a time, frozen in their positions, hardly daring to breathe. Then they would move forward for a few more feet and stop again. It was tedious, and in spite of the danger, they found themselves almost giving way to drowsiness. Alex's head would droop, and he would get a swift kick from Donaldson; then the reverse would happen, with Alex jolting his friend awake. They could hear the closest sentry stamping his feet.

Suddenly there came the sound of a sentry passing close to them. This was followed by a sound that startled them all—a gunshot crackled through the night. It was followed by a shout, then an ominous silence. Five minutes later a German soldier came running by very close to them, panting with effort. He disappeared around a bend to the right. They stayed frozen for another ten minutes, then the guide got up and started moving, waving for them to follow.

All weariness forgotten, they dashed across the clearing to the electric fence. The guide paused only long enough to make sure they were all there, then he bent to the fence. Four snaps, four blue flashes, and the guide was through, waving them frantically beneath the loose wiring. While he was going under the fence the little Belgian, Sew, tried to push the man in front of him, but instead he lost his balance and fell into one of the water-filled trenches. No one understood why he wasn't electrocuted. In his tumble he nearly knocked Alex into the water as well. In a desperate rush the men fled underneath the wires and went on a dead run to a stand of trees in the distance. Tillinghast would later laugh that he was the last one under the wires but the first one to reach the Dutch border, approximately a mile away.

They covered their last mile walking and running, constantly looking back. No one was chasing them. At last they stopped. They were all free men, standing in neutral Holland. They had made it.

Alex and his companions were the first, and perhaps the only, prisoners of war to escape from the Germans by making their way across occupied Belgium. What happened next was anticlimactic: they had to wait for a train.

Now in the town of Weert, they wandered around, waiting for a train to Rotterdam, where they intended to see the American consul. While they sauntered around the town they blew all the money they had on chocolates. At "five dollars a slab," as Alex noted, it didn't take long.

Their guide was still traveling with them, and he bought their tickets to Rotterdam. The train ride was uneventful, and they arrived in Rotterdam at seven in the evening. The next thing they knew, they were being arrested.

Upon leaving the train, they passed a man in a black hat and a long gray overcoat. Suddenly, the man grabbed the guide and asked if the men with him were all Belgians. Next he herded them all together, showed them his police badge, and took them down to headquarters. Without papers of any kind, they were going to be detained at least for the night. Alex and the others lost their tempers and got ready to fight—they hadn't escaped from the Germans only to wind up in a Dutch prison. Before the situation worsened, an English-speaking Dutch police officer stepped in to try to restore calm. The Americans, however, insisted upon speaking to the American consul and would not be denied.

Their fortunes improved immediately. They found an assistant to the consul, who promptly issued them passports and also instructed the Suidhollande Hotel to give them the run of the hotel. This translated into a marvelous dinner and soft beds. In the hotel grill the next day they had lunch with the consul, Colonel Listoe, who both marveled and laughed at their experiences. He outlined their next moves: "You boys will be taken care of at once. This afternoon you will go with Mr. Krow to The Hague, reporting there to Colonel Davis, who is our military attaché. He will give you orders to report to the military attaché in London. Arrangements will be made with the British authorities for you to leave by the first convoy for England." Colonel Listoe had a favor to ask: Would they pose for a picture on the steps of the consulate, beneath the American flag, before they left?

The moment was forever seared into Alex's mind—it was the moment when the realization hit home that he had escaped, that a miracle had taken place, and he was alive and safe:

> We accompanied the Colonel to the Consulate, where we stood with him on the entrance steps under the Stars and Stripes while they snapped a picture. The Dutch people passing by stopped in the street to watch the strange performance. But what did it matter that we were thousands of miles from home? For the moment we forgot the strange faces looking on . . . this was just a bit of home transplanted. We had come once more under the protecting folds of Old Glory.

Alex and his fellow escapees and guide (right). After an adventurous trek across Belgium to freedom, they almost were arrested by a Dutch policeman in neutral Holland.

PART TWO

Remember I gave my Aloha
For as long as the waves meet the sand.
Remember when I said "I love you"
Stars looked down and they understand.
The whispering breeze told the mountains
The flowers and trees seem to know . . .
Remember I gave my Aloha
For as long as the trade winds shall blow.

—from "Remember I Gave My Aloha"
   by R. Alexander Anderson, 1971

Back in Honolulu, the cables began to arrive.

From Ruth, in Washington: "Associated Press from Hague meeting troops. Alexander safe in Holland."

From a U.S. official: "Lt. Robert Alexander Anderson, aviation section, Signal Corps, heretofore reported missing, escaped from German Prison in France and arrived at the Hague, Netherlands. He is well."

From another official: "Alexander Anderson reported safe Holland."

Again from Ruth: "Alexander cabled, safe London."

On November 9 Don Chamberlain of London's United Press told the world about the escape in a dispatch, calling it "a thrilling 24-day flight through occupied Belgium." Alex was quoted extensively, telling the story in straightforward terms, without heroics or histrionics. The story was dramatic enough to get good exposure wherever United Press had newspaper and radio clients.

As if in authentication of Alex's escape and its happy conclusion, Alex's mother received a letter from a merchant in London— a follow-up to an earlier letter that apparently had not taken into consideration the fact that Alex had been shot down and taken prisoner. The second letter was certainly more conciliatory than the first:

> Madame, referring to our letter of the 11th of October regarding the account of your son, 1st Lt. Robert Alexander Anderson, we are delighted to inform you that Lt. Anderson has escaped from Germany and is in excellent health. We had the pleasure of a visit from him today and his account has been placed in order. We therefore regret having troubled you on this matter, and remain yours faithfully, etc.

On November 1 Alex reported to the London headquarters and was promptly sent back to the training squadron at Ayr, Scotland, to lecture—not surprisingly, he was to give pointers to the new cadets on how to escape from the Germans. The assignment was short-lived; at the eleventh hour of the eleventh day of the eleventh month, the armistice brought the war to end all wars to an end.

In Honolulu, Dr. and Mrs. Anderson were relieved and ecstatic. Alex, meanwhile, was ordered to detach from the squadron and to return to the United States. He was already dreaming of the surf at Waikīkī. In early December he boarded the USS *Mauritania*, and after an uneventful crossing, he arrived at Mineola, Long Island, to receive his discharge. He was awarded the World War I Victory Medal and two chevrons, but in the swiftness of his separation from the military, the most important medal he earned was quite overlooked. It was an oversight that would be corrected more than forty years later.

In New York Alex took the opportunity to see his half brother, Francis Ketchum Anderson. Francis entertained Alex at a luncheon with a well-known editor and writer, Charles Hansen Towne, who was then editing the popular *McClure's* magazine. When Towne heard Alex's story, he urged him to write about his escape for the magazine. "I'll probably chop it all to pieces," he warned Alex, "but anyway, we'll see." Alex began the story while he was still in New York, and it turned into a seven-part series in the magazine. Towne didn't chop it up, but Alex received no money for his efforts.

The stories, initiated under the title "The Dawn Patrol," were a huge success. Years later, Alex showed them to a Hollywood screenwriter visiting Hawai'i, who had no scruples about taking the title and some of the incidents for a film that remained popular for years as *The Dawn Patrol*. Again, Alex received no money.

Alex came home on February 1, 1919, to a rousing welcome. When his ship docked, the Punahou band was dockside with a group of ROTC cadets; they all paraded Alex up to 'Iolani Palace, where he was given recognition for his escape. Alex was pleased, but he remained modest about the escape. There were pictures and a story in the local newspapers the next day.

He did not come home alone. On the ship was a fellow flying officer with whom he'd developed a fast friendship. This was Paul Winslow, of Chicago, who was now visiting Hawai'i at Alex's invitation. Alex's sister, Ruth, was also on the ship, and a shipboard romance blossomed as Paul and Ruth saw more and more of each other. Alex couldn't have been more pleased, and later he loved to tell the story of how Paul and Ruth fell in love. Winslow proposed and Ruth accepted; they were married in Central Union Church with Alex as Paul's best man, cementing a closeness that lasted all their lives. Paul took Ruth back to Chicago to live.

Ruth and husband Paul Winslow. They were married in Central Union Church, but lived on the Mainland.

Alex didn't know it then, but Chicago would eventually beckon him as well. For the moment he wanted nothing more than to soak up the sun, get on his surfboard, and catch a wave. But somewhere the fates laughed and sent him Peggy.

Once again, part of the story begins in Scotland. Young David Center was one of those mechanical-minded young Scots who had a great deal of ambition. He turned up in California, much like many a Scotsman wandering far with an eye of bettering himself. He read in a newspaper that Claus Spreckels—long a dominant figure in Hawai'i sugar operations—was planning to open a new plantation in picturesque Hāna, on the windward coast of Maui. Center lost no time in angling for a job on the plantation.

On the ship coming to Hawai'i Center met Flora Allen, who was en route to Hawai'i to visit her best friend, Mrs. Elizabeth Turner, a teacher at Punahou. Suddenly Center found something he wanted more than anything else, and when Flora returned to California after her Hawai'i visit Center followed her back, and before long they were married. Then the couple returned to Hāna and settled down to plantation life. Margaret Leith Center was born August 17, 1895, at Spreckelsville, Maui.

Margaret—Peggy, as she was called—went to Punahou, where here first-grade teacher was Mrs. Elizabeth Turner. Peggy and Alex were two years apart and never really knew each other well in school, although Alex's sister, Ruth, was in Peggy's class, and they became good friends. Peggy remembered those years vividly:

When I went to Punahou, my father had passed away when he was very young, and mother had moved to Honolulu with all her family, a family of six. We lived up on Green Street. Today that's Ward Avenue. She gave me a horse; and this little pony—the name was Robin—and I used to ride over the hills along Thurston Avenue to Wilder with my sister, Helen, three years younger than I, holding around my waist, sitting on

CHAPTER 12

a gunny sack on the back of the saddle. We rode Robin to Punahou School. When we would get out there I would unsaddle him and put the saddle against a kiawe tree—there were big kiawe trees on the campus—and tie him up, and he would eat his way around, eat the kiawe beans and the grass underneath the tree.

It was an idyllic schoolgirl existence. Peggy enjoyed Punahou, with her friends and her French classes, and she particularly enjoyed singing in the Punahou Choir. She was a fun-loving girl, sunny and in love with life. So when she read in a newspaper that Alex and Ruth were returning she and a group of friends went to see them:

We all went into the Anderson home. And Andy had read in the paper in the morning about me and my music [Peggy was performing in a series of local concerts] and he came over and sat down beside me. He didn't look at anybody else. And we sat there and talked music until it was late—simply exciting! And finally I was so smart: I said, "Andy, I think the story of your escape is so thrilling and Honolulu people would love to hear it. Would you be kind enough to come on in the intermission and tell the story of your escape?"

Whereupon my concerts in Honolulu were absolutely filled to the hilt. And when I went to Kaua'i, and he wanted to go with me, I gave a concert over there. Wonderful people, the Mokihana Girls, arranged for the theatre and arranged for the ushers. And from there he went with me to Maui, and I gave a concert on Maui.

Peggy earned five thousand dollars from those concerts, but the important thing was that it was the first partnership between Peggy and Alex, and it was one they both enjoyed.

Music was so much of that partnership, but Peggy's musical career might have lead her away from Alex, and there was a time when their paths might have taken them far from each other. Peggy, in fact, already had traveled far—she had just returned from Australia a few days before Alex arrived back in Hawai'i. It had been an enriching experience, because Peggy was involved with the leading singer of the day, an international star whose own beginnings in music were anything but easy.

The world would come to know here as Dame Melba, but she was born Helen Porter Mitchell on May 19, 1861. From the beginning everyone called her Nellie. Critics praised her for her extraordinary voice, and Oscar

Wilde told her, "Ah, Madame Melba, I am the lord of language and you are the queen of song." (Wilde, a broken and shabby man later in life, came up to her on the streets of Paris and begged for money, whereupon Melba emptied her purse into his hands.)

Young Nellie grew up in Australia, a fey girl who was patient with young creatures, gentle as she stroked a dog's head or calmed a nervous pony. Her granddaughter, Pamela Vestey, remembered her as delighting in country life. Nellie's mother, however, often lost patience with Nellie for singing about the house all the time and often ordered her to "stop that humming."

After the death of her mother and younger sister, Nellie went to Queensland for a holiday. There she met Charles Armstrong, the son of an Irish baronet. Their subsequent marriage was not a success, and she was soon back in Melbourne, where she sang in public for the first time, at the Melbourne town hall. Not surprisingly, the critics predicted a great career for her. Nellie was delighted when her father was transferred to a job in England, and she attempted a singing career in Europe. After a poorly attended concert in Paris, she met Madame Marchesi, a famous teacher, and began studying in earnest.

Nellie's confidence was shaken. She had been given a lukewarm reception in England, and she was a questionable personality for sophisticated Parisians, who noted that she was from a supposedly barbaric country and that she was now trailed by a daughter but no attendant husband. But Nellie was quick-witted and determined, and she persisted. Her granddaughter remarked that "doors opened before her, and if they didn't, she pushed them."

Madame Marchesi changed Nellie's name to Melba and launched her in Brussels in the role of Gilda in "Rigoletto." The Belgians told her, "You're wonderful!" and over the next thirty years Dame Melba became a household word. She sang before Queen Victoria and traveled in glittering social circles. In Russia, people threw their coats in the snow to protect her feet. In Venice, when she sang in a gondola just for fun, people threw money. In America, Oscar Hammerstein scattered money around her hotel room to persuade her to make an American tour, and she took Chicago, New York, and San Francisco by storm. In San Francisco she was engaged to sing in Rossini's *The Barber of Seville*, which was not a wise choice at a time when America was on the brink of war with Spain. The audience was hostile, but in the second act there was a scene portraying a singing lesson, in which Melba could sing any song she wanted. She brought the audience to its feet, cheering, when she sang "The Star-Spangled Banner."

This woman, truly a legendary figure, was invited to a dinner in Honolulu at the home of Mr. and Mrs. Walter Dillingham. Peggy was invited to attend with Melba's pianist, Frank St. Leger. Peggy was thrilled to meet Madame Melba, but she had no great expectations. Then St. Leger asked her, "Peggy, do you play the piano?" Peggy never forgot the ensuing events:

I said, "I play the piano very badly, but I want to sing. I want to go to the Boston Conservatory of Music." And he said, "Have you a voice?" And I said, "I don't know. I play the guitar and I sing songs that all the kids are singing today, and I play and sing." I said I was in the community theatre and that "I would love to be able to sing." He said, "Bring some music tomorrow morning to Bergstrom Music Company"—which in those days was on the corner of King and Fort Street. He said, "Melba will be going in to see her manager, Mr. Adams, about her concert she is giving." And I said, "Oh, Mr. Adams is a great friend of my mother's, she always signs up for the concerts in the old Royal Hawaiian Opera House." So I said, "I'd love to do that."

So I went home and told my mother. I could hardly sleep, I was so excited. He was going to hear me sing and tell me whether I should go on with singing.

The next morning mother said, "I'm going with you." We went to Bergstrom Music Store and Melba came in. I didn't know she was coming and I was terrified when I saw her. She looked at me and said, "Peggy, I met you last night and I understand you're going to sing for me." I said, "Oh, no, I'm going to sing for Frank." She said, "Well, you're going to sing for me, too, because I want to hear you."

We went upstairs to this room and there was a piano there. Frank put my sheet music on the piano and began playing when Melba interrupted and said, "Peggy, I want to hear you sing. Have you ever had lessons?" No. "All right," she said, "you do what I tell you." She used to be a very good pianist, so she sat down and started with the key of C and said "I'm going to have you sing, ah! You do that all the way through." She started with C and went all the way up the scale. She went up to F, and I was singing ah! all the way . . . I went up so high. F is very high. And she turned around and said, "That's wonderful. You've never had a lesson? I'm leaving next Friday on the *Niagara*, going back to Australia. I'm going to be there all during the war. I want you as my protégé. You're going with me and I'm going to teach you." I nearly died. My mother cried. We all had a time crying with joy.

So I went to Australia and spent three wonderful years with that beautiful woman. I earned my own way, giving concerts here and there. In those days I was paid 50 guineas a night for a little concert program. The Governor General of Australia and his wife I met through Melba, and when they would have a VIP party, they would put on a little program and let me sing. I made 50 guineas a night and it helped me to stay the three years in Australia.

Then when the war was over, she wanted to go right back to London, and she was planning to take me with her. We were planning a concert in Honolulu but when we got as far as Auckland, New Zealand, all the theatres were closed because of the wretched flu that was in the Pacific in 1919, and everybody was sick with it wherever we went. So we sent a cable to Honolulu, wanting a concert while the ship was in port but the message came back . . . all the theatres were closed indefinitely on account of the flu. So I told Madame Melba I would have to get off and start giving concerts because I had to help my mother keep me in my career.

So she went on her way, and I saw her sail away and I cried and she cried. She said, "I'll get to London and open my flat and you'll be with me. And then I will take you to Paris and put you in with a *répititeur* to learn French opera.

Alex remembered the early days of his relationship with Peggy well:

Some of Ruth's friends were coming to call on her and probably with more intention of meeting Paul, the newcomer. And Peggy went along. So, in the course of the visit, we started talking together about her music and what I had been doing. I felt a strong attraction and in the following days, dated her to go various places. At the same time, Paul was very attentive to Ruth and the four of us in mother's little Chandler roadster, took many trips around the Island together, swimming at windward side beaches and picnicking and having a generally delightful time, all of us enjoying each other.

On the ship from Australia, there was an English Captain go-

rated in Alex's makeup. Remembering the time he'd been asked if being a salesman was demeaning (he had replied emphatically that it was honest work), he later told an interviewer that the job demanded certain qualities: "personality, enthusiasm, endurance, stick-to-itivness, sincerity and honesty, a thorough belief in the product one is selling." He never felt that any work was beneath him.

A family member recalls that Alex could always find time to fit a little recreation into the course of his day. In fact, Alex always seemed to be on the golf course just prior to his children being born, so that Peggy, in their Pacific Heights home overlooking the Oʻahu Country Club, would signal the impending delivery by hanging a sheet over the balcony. (It was not reported whether Alex left for home immediately or played through in the manner of dedicated golfers).

"He was a great sportsman," recalls his daughter, Pam.

He loved the water, loved to sail. He was a good yachtsman and represented Hawaiʻi in the 1930s in the Star boat class races back on Lake Ponchartrain, Louisiana, and he was Commodore of the Pearl Harbor Yacht Club. But in sailing with him, it was always a lot of fun because he had something humorous to say and comments on the beauties of Hawaiʻi as we sailed along the coast of Waikīkī, racing.

And in traveling all over the world with him—even back to the area where he was stationed in World War I, and playing golf on the course at Turnberry where he flew his practice runs—he was an awful lot of fun to be around. He had a great memory and a great kindness for other people. And behind him was my mother, who was such a great part of his life. The two of them were inseparable.

Allen Anderson remembered how busy his father always was:

I was raised under the continuing supervision of my mother, with the occasional assistance of Dad. He worked. He golfed. (He did teach us to play golf.) He went on business trips to America. He belonged to—and sooner or later was president of—almost every private club and business group there was. This didn't keep him at home very much, although he was home for dinner every night that he and mother were not out at a dinner party. They were pretty

The minister was highly complimentary of Peggy's signing—he had heard her in concert in Honolulu—but Jean interrupted him: "Dean Ault, would you please take Peggy and have a talk with her? She needs to talk to somebody like you." Peggy explained, "Well, I'm so much in love that I don't think I am going on with my career." Dean Ault nodded, and after breakfast he took Peggy aside.

"I said to Dean Ault," Peggy remembered, "that I felt so dreadful because I owed so much to Madame Melba. I owed so much to the people of Honolulu and the Islands, and I owed so much to my dear mother, and I couldn't bear hurting anybody. But I loved Andy—as I called him."

Dean Ault replied, "He's such a fine young man, Peggy, you couldn't do anything more wonderful. I'm going to tell you something. You must not say you owe so much to people. What you do, you owe to your own life and the life of that young man. You must make up your mind and not keep dilly-dallying."

Peggy called Madame Melba, who rose to the occasion with magnanimity: "You only have the love of a great man once in your life. Go ahead and marry him."

That night was a sleepless one for Peggy. She paced and thought, and finally she made her decision. There were no long-distance telephones, so she wrote Alex a letter explaining her decision. Then she sent him a telegram. She was coming back to Chicago, she told him, and they would be married.

Alex was overjoyed. Paul and Ruth were also delighted, and they began to help arrange the wedding. Paul's parents wanted to have the reception after the wedding, which would take place at the Christ Church in Chicago, with the rector performing the ceremony. By the time Peggy reached Chicago, the arrangements were set.

"Meanwhile," Alex recalled,

I had started the job with ISKO, so, not wanting to take off a lot of time right at the start—it might prejudice them against me—we decided to have the wedding on a Saturday and our honeymoon at the Edgewater Hotel on Sunday and I report to work as usual Monday morning. This was a tough thing to do, but I had no choice, having just taken the job.

I looked for an apartment I could afford and found one for

$100 a month way out on Roby Street at the northwest end of Chicago. The $100 a month was against my salary of $300 a month, so we knew we would have to be frugal in our other expenses, which we did. Paul also had a job with ISKO and it must have been better than mine because they moved into a much plusher apartment than we had, in the neighborhood of his parents, the fashionable part of town.

I think back to the wedding and how sweet it was. The little church was filled with Winslow's family and friends. After the service, the Winslow seniors had the reception for us in their home. Aside from them, Ruth, Paul, and Jean (who was Peggy's matron of honor), we didn't know any of the nice people who came and congratulated us. It was a very nice affair. I remember my bride in a brown suit (it seems to me it was silk) carrying a bouquet of yellow roses. She was adorable, the prettiest bride that ever was.

After the reception, Peggy and I went to the Edgewater Hotel right on Lake Michigan, on the north side of the city, a lovely hotel. I remember having dinner while one of the orchestras of that time—I don't remember whose—was playing music for dancing. It was a delightful honeymoon for two days, after which I reported for work on Monday morning. Peggy was very understanding and in fact was always understanding of the things that had to be done, although not always what we would prefer to do. Jean left us to return to Honolulu after saying our farewells and thanking her for taking such good care of my bride.

Alex and Peggy were married on November 14, 1919, and they moved into their third-floor apartment. Their first Christmas was one they would always remember:

Peggy had trimmed a tree and done all kinds of nice surprise things to welcome me when I came home from work. I had to follow a string from the front door leading all over the apartment until it finally arrived at the little tree. This was Christmas Eve. There was snow on the ground outside but the little apartment was well heated and we were cozy as we celebrated Christmas coming, although we had nothing, you might say. There were checks from home with which to buy china, glassware, and silverware, which we subsequently did, and we bought the best brands.

Alex and Peggy were to keep those early acquisitions for seventy years.

The newlyweds were happy in spite of their need to pinch pennies. "I used to take the elevated back and forth to work," Alex remembered, "and Peggy was on foot in the area, doing the daily shopping. Later, with a generous check from home, we bought a used Oldsmobile, a five-seater with open sides, just a top and curtains to hook on the sides for winter driving."

But in its second year, ISKO failed. Some said that there was a mechanical defect in the compressor mechanism, and others claimed that there was a problem with the gas used in the machine. About a month after they were sold, the machines began coming back to the factory.

Alex had become interested in refrigeration and its potential, and he wanted to continue in the field. He was able to secure a job with another company, the McClelland Refrigerating Company, and move on with his experience in refrigeration in Chicago. The months and then the years slid into an easy rhythm.

Chicago was anything but dull for the Andersons in the early 1920s. It was the era of Prohibition, when alcoholic beverages were forbidden and mobsters cashed in on the propensity of Americans to find a drink when they wanted one. Illegal sales and "bathtub gin" were common, and Prohibition boosted the sales of soft drinks and sodas. It was the time of the Chicago White Sox scandal, in which eight members of the team were indicted for fraud in a World Series loss to Cincinnati. The National Football League was organized, a principal figure of which was George Halas, who became owner of the Chicago Bears.

Of interest to Alex was an innovation in aviation—General Billy Mitchell led a mass bombing attack on a former German battleship to prove that air power would make large naval vessels obsolete. Soon a Navy collier was converted into the Navy's first aircraft carrier, the USS *Langley*. Alex remained an avid follower of developments in aviation.

Chicago's Field Museum of Natural History, founded in 1893, opened a new building overlooking Grant Park. In the world of music, to which both Alex and Peggy paid attention, Sergei Rachmaninoff presented his new Concerto No. 3 for Piano and *Orchestra in the Windy City*, and a new opera debuted in Chicago—*The Love for Three Oranges*, by Sergei Prokofiev.

The most exciting event for the Andersons was the birth of a son in 1921, named Robert A. Anderson, Jr. Alex progressed with his new company, and before long he was promoted to chief engineer. Life was comfortable enough as his salary improved, and Alex and Peggy began to seem like a typical American couple making their way in a great American city. But Hawai'i was never far from their thoughts.

There were letters from home to remind them of the very things Alex would later write about in songs—soft green seas, fragrant evenings, and the moonlight on Diamond Head. Even without the letters, Hawai'i was there in their consciousness as the "Alohaland" that Alex had praised in his first hit song. Chicago was interesting and full of promise, but Hawai'i was home.

The Andersons went back to Hawai'i for a visit in 1923, possibly with an eye for opportunities in the islands. One turned up that was like a dream come true, and it came from a gruff old German born in 1870 in Bremen, who ended up in Hawai'i because of a stamp collection.

Conrad Von Hamm was employed by a bank in Bremen when he fell into an exchange of correspondence with his cousin, William Maertens, because both men were interested in stamp collecting.

The old Von Hamm-Young headquarters. Entrepreneur Alexander Young was Alex's grandfather, and Alex held a life-long admiration for the old Scots' achievements.

Maertens was senior partner in the importing firm of Hoffschlaeger and Company, in Honolulu. Their mutual interest in stamps led to Von Hamm's arrival in Honolulu to take a post in Maertens' company. Von Hamm worked out so well that a decade later he was offered a full partnership in the company, but instead he decided to launch his own business in partnership with Archibald Young and Archibald's impressive father, Alexander Young.

The company was called Von Hamm-Young Company, and it was hardly launched before a fire in 1900 that destroyed much of Honolulu's Chinatown also wiped out a lot of their inventory. The company rebounded, importing automobiles, and a few years later they launched a series of garages with branches on Maui, Kaua'i, and Hawai'i Island. When Conrad Von Hamm offered Alex a job, Von Hamm was just two years away from becoming president of the company. He would go on to become chairman and retire in 1958 with a fortune of some $20 million.

Von Hamm was not only a highly respected and successful businessman; he was family. In 1898, he married Ida Bernice Young, a daughter of Alexander Young. Thus he was Alex's uncle.

"Don't you think," asked Von Hamm, in his heavily accented German, "it is time you came back to Hawai'i to work for Von Hamm-Young?" Alex could not have agreed more.

The Andersons came back from Chicago, and Alex brought two important items back with him. The first was a franchise from Frigidaire for Von Hamm-Young to distribute in Hawai'i, and the second was a song in his head that expressed his feelings for the islands. "Haole Hula," he called it, and the lyrics said, "I love to dance and sing the charms of Hawai'i . . . for then I know you'll be in love with them too."

The song was, perhaps, Alex's favorite. It was the first of his songs to be recorded, and a well-known dancer, Winona Love, improvised a dance and introduced the song to the mainland with a performance in the Biltmore Hotel in Los Angeles.

Meanwhile, Alex was making his presence felt at Von Hamm-Young. Decades later, he recalled to an interviewer:

When the Alexander Young Hotel was operating, it had a tank in the basement for making ice. That got me interested in smaller packages of ice and something for the home. [Frigidaire] had a new machine for householders and I told my uncle, Mr. Von Hamm, that this little Frigidaire machine was taking hold in California and I thought we could do a lot with it. He was making a trip to San Francisco and I had to meet with the San Francisco representative of Frigidaire on my way home. My uncle called on him and we signed a subdealer contract and we got our first Frigidaire out here [in Hawai'i]. The first machines came out here all boxed in—after a while they learned to ship with just an open create the way that most things come out here these days.

When people saw how it was they started buying them. Before long, everybody wanted one. It went over very well.

Shortly after that, Jack Reilly, from one of the big houses in San Francisco, was engaged to come down and run the McInerny store on Merchant and Fort Street. He was coming out of San Francisco and the first day on the job he told me, "I can't stand this climate." I told him, "We can cool the store with a refrigeration unit," and that was our first store installation. We cooled him off.

Von Hamm-Young furnished the refrigeration equipment for the Royal Hawaiian Hotel, and Alex was in charge of the project. Still, Conrad Von Hamm had misgivings about Alex's songwriting efforts. Early in his career at Von Hamm-Young, Alex was cornered by Conrad Von Hamm, who growled, "Alexander, I think you are not attending to business. You're writing songs."

Alex remembered, "He got me riled up for a moment. But I happened to know that he and his wife enjoyed playing bridge. I knew they played two or three evenings a week. So I said, 'Uncle Conrad, I happen to know your hobby is playing bridge. My hobby is songwriting. In the evening when you're playing three or four hours of bridge, I can write a song. When I'm on the job, I'm tending to business."
Von Hamm never bothered Alex about songwriting again.

CHAPTER 13

The songs were germinating, and soon they began to appear. After "Haole Hula" came "Lei, Lei Buy Lei," which Alex wrote with Don Blanding. This was followed by "Honeymoon Isle," which he wrote with Flora J. Center. With abundant energy, Alex found himself involved with the company founded by his grandfather, the Alexander Young Company, which owned the Royal Hawaiian Hotel, the Moana Hotel, and the landmark Alexander Young Hotel. In the 1920s Alex was part of the planning process that resulted in cottages being added to the Moana property and the Seaside Hotel. (The Moana was in fee, but the Seaside was on Bishop Estate leasehold, and the lease expired in 1926, when Matson became the successful bidder for the renewal.)

Alex's Punahou class had held its graduation dance in the Moana's dining room, and as he worked on the cottages he often thought of the nights when he would hear Hawaiian serenaders on the nearby pier and on the beach alongside the pier. He always recalled those nights with a quiet pleasure. Others wondered when Alex had time for nostalgia, for he was beginning his long years of community service, starting in an area in which he had undoubted expertise: on June 21, 1929, he was appointed chairman of the Territorial Aeronautics Commission, to succeed Colonel Perry M. Smoot, whose commission was expiring on July 5.

A local newspaper carried a photo of Alex sitting in an airplane at John Rodgers Airport (which became Honolulu International Airport). Alex wore a flying cap and goggles, perhaps in hopes that he would get to fly again, and he did. The aircraft took off, piloted by Walter B. Cannon, chief pilot for Hawaiian Aeronautical Industries, but Alex was allowed to

Alex and Peggy were among the arrivals in Kailua-Kona on one of Inter-Islands' first flights among the islands.

take the controls for a while. It was the first time he'd flown since the armistice in 1918.

His appointment could hardly have come at a more interesting time for aviation in the islands. Less than six months later, on November 11, 1929, commercial interisland air service began when Inter-Island Airways launched its inaugural flight. The company, which later became Hawaiian Airlines, employed two Sikorsky amphibian aircraft and sent one of them on a historic flight to Hilo on the Big Island, with a stopover at Maui's Māʻalaea Field. Operating from John Rodgers Airport, the company also began scheduled flights to Molokaʻi. The day after its inaugural flight, the company began scheduled air service to Kauaʻi, with two flights weekly to Port Allen.

Other expansions came quickly. In 1930 Inter-Island Airways began service to Lānaʻi, flying in and out of a field owned by the Hawaiian Pineapple Company. Prison labor was used to extend runways on Kauaʻi and Maui, and in 1931 an airstrip was started at Wailua on Kauaʻi with an appropriation of thirty thousand dollars.

Alex was involved in these burgeoning aviation activities, and at the same time he was moving up in his company. When he was appointed chairman of the Aeronautics Commission he was treasurer of Von Hamm-Young Company. His workload was increasing, and there was a hiatus in his songwriting efforts. But this did not last long. In 1934, 1935, and 1936, he copyrighted ten songs, including two that would remain perennial favorites, "Soft Green Seas," written with Leonie Weeks, and the rollicking "Cockeyed Mayor of Kaunakakai."

One of the songs from that era, "Reach Up and Pick a Star," was written out of pure sentiment. The Alexander Young Hotel had opened a roof garden for music and dancing, and Alex thought that from that vantage point the stars seemed so close, you could touch them. "Reach up and pick a star," he wrote, "you can touch one where you are." The roof garden became famous for its "dress up" affairs with dancing to the music of Giggie Royce and his band. In 1936 Alex was instrumental in bringing Del Courtney and his band to the roof garden, and Courtney's music enlivened the local scene for years.

If Alex was surprised by the success of "Cockeyed Mayor," he also was bemused by some of its ramifications. He had written the song when actor Warner Baxter was on Moloka'i making a film. Baxter and his role more or less inspired the song, and Alex wrote it in innocence, only to learn that the CBS, NBC, and ABC radio stations all refused to play it. They claimed that the song made fun of mayors and ridiculed people who had such a deformity as being cockeyed. None of this had occurred to Alex, who never wrote anything out of malice, and he was shocked by the networks' attitude. For Alex it was simply a comedic tune.

The networks changed their attitude in time, particularly when a talented comedian-dancer with the stage name of Hilo Hattie took a fancy to the song. It suited her flamboyant talents perfectly. "She must have danced it a thousand times in New York alone," Alex recalled. Hilo Hattie, born Clarissa Haili, was a teacher turned entertainer, and for some thirty years she was a familiar sight in her coconut hat and mu'umu'u, entertaining with her husband, Carlyle Nelson, and his band at the Roosevelt Hotel in Los Angeles. She also appeared in several films. She and her husband remained friends of Alex and Peggy's throughout their lifetimes.

On April 4, 1924, Alex and Peggy celebrated the birth of their second child. David Leith Anderson came into the world in his mother's bed in the Anderson house at 2940 Pacific Heights Road, a picturesque home that cantilevered out over the southeastern wall of Nuʻuanu Valley. It had ample room, and it also permitted the family to have various pets, including dogs, ducks, guinea pigs, and pigeons. Once a baby lamb arrived, courtesy of Kahuā Ranch on the Big Island. The lamb was cute and cuddly but soon grew into a regulation-sized ram and had to be sent back to the ranch.

There were plenty of children in the neighborhood, and Alex and Peggy saw no reason not to add to their brood. On March 30, 1926, a third son was born in exactly the same place as David Leith had been. He was named Allen Willis Anderson. David Leith had been named for his maternal grandfather, and Allen Willis was named for his paternal grandfather. When the Anderson's fourth child was born on March 19, 1931, Alex and Peggy were delighted to have a daughter to add to the family, and they named her Pamela Susan, after Pamela Vestey, the granddaughter of Dame Nellie Melba.

Life was pleasant. Alex had his career with Von Hamm-Young and his songs. In addition, his position in the community kept expanding, and he became the leader of, or at least joined, almost every worthy cause and community project. His community positions demanded his presence not only during the day but also in the evenings, so that the children saw less of him than they wanted to. Alex was becoming a sportsman as well, with a keen interest in sailing and golfing and more than a passing interest in photography and carpentry. His engineer's eye was easily focused on new gadgets and their uses. He was the kind of man who could get twenty-five hours of activity out of a twenty-four-hour day, and if the children had any complaint about him, it was that he was frequently absent.

Alex did have time to take the children to school most days, first to Hanahauʻoli and later to Punahou. Even while he was driving the children, Alex sometimes seemed far away. "He was usually silent," remembers one of the children, "because either the lyrics or the music of a new tune were going through his head." Nevertheless, the children often were treated to a laugh at Anderson's jocularity. "His sense of humor and his quick wit" are recalled by one son:

> I can remember . . . when we were all likely to be talking together, for example, at the dinner table, he would often make a play on words out of what someone else had said, or make a joke, or turn an incident into something to laugh at. Sometimes he was driving in the car when it seemed he was not paying attention, he would make

us all laugh by the same technique. I don't mean to suggest it was planned behavior. It was purely spontaneous . . . I think evidence of this is found in some of his songs.

Life was pleasant, in part, because of the climate of innocence and the easygoing lifestyle of prewar Hawai'i, when the population of the islands was less than four hundred thousand, the roads were unclogged, the trade winds were unobstructed by high-rises, and the tempos of both business and leisure were slow. In those days visitors to Hawai'i tended to arrive prepared for a lengthy visit—some of the more affluent even brought their own cars. Boat days were events that called for lei, bands, champagne, and youngsters diving for coins alongside the big ships. Hawai'i had an aura that projected an image of magic, of gentle days and languorous evenings and romance under the stars.

Life in Hawai'i was especially rewarding for young people. The romance was there, of course, to be enjoyed with the scent of flowers and the sound of the surf breaking on the reef. During the day there were picnics, surfing, and swimming; evenings brought strolls under a great yellow Hawaiian moon. It was the "Alohaland" that Alex had missed at Cornell, and now he was living the dream. He was not so mature that he couldn't feel the poignant romance of the islands, and with collaborator George Hopkins he wrote one of his least-known but most romantic songs, "Love Song in the Night." It went, in part: "Gently from slumber wakening, longing you brought to me / Longing and ecstasy came to me with a love song in the night."

If Alex had a romantic streak, it never got in the way of his work. He continued to be an officer in the Alexander Young company, and he handled the local distribution of manufacturers' products from many places on the mainland. He was responsible for introducing not only Frigidaire to Hawai'i, but also many other brand-name products that filled needs in the islands—products such as Zenith radios, Otis elevators, Cummins engines, Dodge automobiles, and that mainstay of many sugar plantations, heavy-duty off-road cane-haul trucks. His decisions were usually right on target, but in one instance he made a horrendous mistake that he was able to laugh about later: "I was offered the Hawai'i distribution for Volkswagen automobiles. I thought it was the ugliest car I'd ever seen and would never be popular. I turned down the offer!" Von Hamm-Young did get the Datsun (now Nissan) distributorship, however, and the company did very well with it.

There was an old-fashioned and very Scottish work ethic incorpo-

ing back to England. He and Peggy saw a lot of each other during the trip from Australia to Honolulu and he chose to get off in Honolulu to see more of her before she went on to Europe. While we were enjoying each other's company, he tried to get dates and Peggy put him off most of the time in order to go out with me. We took moonlight rides and our favorite ride was up the Tantalus Road about halfway where we like to park, with the car heading down and looking over the city and out to Diamond Head.

One moonlight night I couldn't wait any longer and I told Peggy I loved her. She said she was growing fond of me and that we were happy going together. A night or two later I proposed to her, saying at the same time that I knew she was pursuing a career and I didn't want to be the one to stop it. So I suggested we be engaged and she go on with her plans while I would get a job which had been offered to me in Chicago by a company in which Paul's father had stock. We agreed to wait for each other and I would come for her at a future date after I had established myself in the new job.

We were very much in love and were regretful of the waiting we would have to do before we could be married, but decided it was the best plan and she would proceed to Madame Melba in London by the next ship. I felt that if I had persuaded her to give up her career and be married she would always hold it against me. So in spite of the hardship, this was the best way to proceed.

Alex went off to Chicago to take up his new position with a firm called ISKO, where Paul Winslow also was employed. Alex was, at last, ready to put his engineering skills to use. His firm manufactured a machine that was designed to fit into the ice compartment of old-fashioned iceboxes. Peggy also went to Chicago, but only as a stopover on her way to New York, from where she would go on to Europe to continue her studies and her musical career. In Chicago, Peggy realized how much she and Alex were in love. "Separation was going to be hard," she said, "but I was determined to go ahead with my career, and I went to New York for two days . . . I was booked to sail on the *Baltic* on November 19, 1919."

Peggy was accompanied in New York by her older sister, Jean. One morning the two girls went down to the hotel dining room for breakfast, where they ran into the Reverend William Ault of Saint Andrew's Cathedral in Honolulu. The girls invited Reverend Ault to have breakfast with them.

social, as required by their status in the community.

Going out to dinner party in prewar Hawai'i often meant going out in a jacket and tie. "They were quite formal," Pam Anderson remembers.

> Mostly he wore coat and tie . . . he did wear *aloha* shirts as temperatures changed and more and more people wore them because there were more buildings, more heat. He loved to go to parties . . . they loved to go to parties together because they did the entertaining. They loved to give of themselves, as a pair. Mother had a lovely voice, trained as an opera singer and knew the proper way to sing. Both their voices held up over the years; they sounded very good together.

They were, of course, singing some of Anderson's songs. Arriving at those songs was a process that Alex used to chuckle over, for it struck him as being, probably, quite different from the way most songwriters worked. First, there was the tune that hung around in his mind for a time. If the tune lingered in his memory long enough, he would figure out one-finger melodies on a piano, then he would finally write the music. Before a song got into final form he would sing it for Peggy, and if she had suggestions for refining the music or rewriting some of the lyrics, Alex listened to her. "I sing every new song for Peggy," he told a friend. He was pleased with the fact that Peggy then became the first to sing his songs and make them popular.

Many of his songs began with a title—a word or phrase that he heard and that stayed with him. The word or words had a rhythm that suggested a theme, and the melody followed. After that he wrote the lyrics. It was not unusual for Alex to knock out a tune in a couple of hours, but then he could spend a month or more working on it, polishing it by finding a better word here or making a small change in the melody there. His wife was, he said, "my best judge and my best critic. Whenever she has said 'Well, I don't think so,' sure enough, changes have made it better."

Every new song added to Alex's store of experience. In 1925 he collaborated with poet Don Blanding to do a revue called *Tropic Topics* for the Junior League. It was produced at the Princess Theatre, and it was a smash hit. It all came about because Alex was already being recognized as a songwriter. A few years later, when actress Mary Pickford came to visit

Hawai'i, she was presented with a ginger lei and promptly remarked that she hadn't heard any songs about this lovely flower. The results were Alex's "White Ginger Blossoms" and a continuing friendship with the actress and her husband. In a letter dated August 17, 1937, Mary Pickford wrote to Alex, "Thanks for the beautiful flowers. You don't need to remind us of Hawai'i; Bud and I have thought of little else. We cannot get the memory of its beauties and the many friends we made there out of our minds, nor do we want to. . . ."

The Anderson children sometimes witnessed Alex's creative juices flowing. Allen Anderson recalls, "I remember him at the piano with a Camel cigarette hanging out of the corner of his mouth or burning in the ash tray. It was at those times that he put his music on paper. During those times we were welcome to listen and/or watch, but do not disturb. Any session could last for one to two hours." (Alex once talked to an interviewer about smoking: "I smoked. I've forgotten when I quit. I think I must have been thirty or maybe even forty. One day I discovered I was chain-smoking, one after another and I said, 'Hey, this isn't good, I don't want to be hooked this way,' so I just quit cold at that time.")

He was a social drinker. "I drank a fair amount as a young person," he said when he was ninety, "but I was always able to get myself home. But I drink very little nowadays . . . I don't frown on drinking, drinking in moderation is okay." At the same time he pointed out that he'd lived a long time because of exercise. "All my life I've been active one way or another. Even today I do sitting-up exercises in the morning, enough to get myself stirred up, to get deep breathing. . . . I've played golf all my life. In my thirties and forties and fifties I played quite a lot of tennis. And I've always been swimming. So I think that's responsible for good health."

In the late 1930s Alex was still in very good health, and he was involved in many areas, as was his nature. In 1938 Peggy sang the lead role in Gilbert and Sullivan's *Mikado*, a production of the community theatre, and Alex happily sang the part of Koko. He knew, now, that music would always be a big part of his life, and he was especially thrilled in 1939 when he was accepted into ASCAP—the American Society of Composers, Authors, and Publishers. This seemed to validate his music, and it added to his string of affiliations, which was growing year by year.

The music revealed Alex's various moods. "Red 'Ōpū," written in 1935, was a warning to sun worshipers:

What am I going to do with my red ‘ōpū?
It's so very sore I don't know what to do . . .
Listen my little sisters, just look at all my blisters,
Let them be a warning to you.

Another comedic tune was "Malihini Mele," in which Alex poked gentle fun at the way newcomers to the islands often misused Hawaiian words and phrases:

As I strolled along the shore, in a mu‘umu‘u made of koa
While I played a tune on my sweet ‘ōkolehao,
And I sang a pretty song as she danced her sweet kapu
With a wikiwiki smile and a nui nui holokū.

After Clare Boothe (who would marry magazine founder Henry Luce and later become a U.S. ambassador) remarked that she had never heard a song about Hawai‘i's volcanoes, Alex, still in a comedic mood, wrote "I Had to Lova and Leava on the Lava":

She came from Kula and did a wicked hula,
On the slopes of Haleakalā;
Her dance volcanic would throw me in a panic,
I thought the girl would slip a hip too far.

He told a friend, "almost anything can inspire me. It can be a catchy line, a good title, or some subject." Another tune from the period shows that Alex was not always in a mood for laughs. "Soft Green Seas" was to become a favorite of many, its plaintive air and hint of sadness conjuring up an image of love and loss in the tropics:

Soft green seas, a mass of leis, flaming trees and lazy days,
Fragrant nights of song and flowers, melting lights and
dream-filled hours,
Smiles and glances, steel guitars, hula dances,
And then to haunt this soul of mine,
Someone, someone left behind.

"Soft Green Seas" proved to be durable. Written with Leonie Weeks, it was one of Anderson's songs that were performed decades later by a British orchestra. The massed voices and orchestral sound made for a memorable performance. It became an album much appreciated later by President Richard Nixon, who expressed his appreciation to Alex in a letter.

CHAPTER 14

Life in the Anderson household was typical of Hawai'i before the war, although it was enlivened by the presence of various pets, as Pam Anderson remembers:

> We had pets . . . not cats, but dogs. In those days cocker spaniels were quite popular, and I was sent off to obedience school to learn to train cocker spaniels. At one time we had a monkey named Mike that someone gave us . . . some people getting a divorce left us Mike, a wonderful little spider monkey, an absolute character. We had a bantam rooster that used to chase the mailman.
>
> When we lived for a time in Kailua one of the people at Von Hamm-Young gave dad a baby pig; Petunia grew to be a thousand pounds (not really), but I absolutely adored that pig and she adored me and whenever I was upset or felt the brothers were too much for me I'd run to Petunia and we'd lie down and she'd oink to me and I'd put my arms around her neck. Brother Bob had a horse over there—there weren't too many houses along Kailua Beach then. I remember we had a wire-haired terrier, other dogs when we moved to Mākālei Place. Dad wasn't wild about pets, it was more mother and me. Bob was a big animal lover, Leith and Allen not so much.

The Andersons bought the Kailua house as a country home, but Alex found that the forty-five-minute drive into town to get to work—this was before the Pali tunnels were constructed to make commuting easier—

was more time on the road than he cared for. So the family only went to Kailua on weekends, and they eventually sold the house.

The Andersons had an uncanny propensity for accidentally coming into contact with celebrities. Pam Anderson remembers knowing a soon-to-be celebrity who had an unpleasant experience on Kailua Beach. She was a precocious little girl of seven or eight, slightly older than Pam, and during a day on the beach she was stung by a Portuguese man-of-war. Her family whisked her away immediately. Years later, at a cocktail party in Honolulu, Pam asked Shirley Temple Black if she remembered being stung on the beach, and she certainly did.

Music continued to be a family affair. Pamela played guitar, 'ukulele and accordion, and she remembers that "one brother played steel guitar, one played drums, one played saxophone, clarinet, and trombone— Allen played the three instruments and was with the first Dixiecrats Group." Allen continued to play professionally for years. "We all had piano lessons," he recalled,

> but I also taught myself to play Bob's clarinet, which he had thrown with disgust into a closet. Then I had some lessons on the alto saxophone, which started me on the road to playing jazz and the big band music of the forties. During my last Honolulu assignment with Standard Oil Company of California (now Chevron) I started playing professionally part-time. My daytime employers never complained about my professional music activity.

The children were also involved with Alex's songwriting, as Pam remembers: "I'd come home and find dad at the piano and mother sitting on the couch and she'd say, "Sit down, Dad has a new song and I want you to hear it." He was playing it and I'd say something about not liking something in there, and mother said "That's exactly what I told him," so immediately he just revised it. Because of her career she was able to help him.

Peggy handled most of the children's routine discipline, with assistance from Alex when it was deemed necessary, which was not all that often. "He never overdisciplined," Pam remembers,

> I think the boys got it a little bit but I was the last one to come along, and we did so many things together there was just no reason

for discipline. He never talked about expecting good grades from us . . . but he wanted all four of us to have an Eastern education, as he had, because he was aware of the transition coming to Hawai'i and he felt the Eastern experience would be very important. He loved Hawai'i and wanted us to appreciate it.

Neither one of them—dad and mother—were very tough. They always wanted to teach manners . . . manners were very important to them, taking care of other people, trying to be conscious of other people's needs. I think it was a sign of the times.

I believe dad always thought we'd come along the way we did, but he was a one of a kind human being. He didn't do things you'd get mad at him for; he didn't have those ups and downs from temper, he was an even keel sort of human being.

The Anderson clan was fortunate to be free of sibling rivalry. Although their age differences kept them apart from time to time, the three brothers and Pam enjoyed each other and appreciated each other's talents. Perhaps Alex and Peggy inspired the relaxed atmosphere: "They used to say that if they ever had a disagreement they never went to bed without settling it," Pam remembers. "If they had quarrels, they had them in private . . . you never heard them haranguing each other in the house."

Alex's unique outlook on life came from a combination of his own stable family background and his experiences in World War I. His experiences gave him a tolerance for other people's foibles, and they gave him an even deeper appreciation for Hawai'i and its lifestyle. He sensed the changes that were coming to Hawai'i, and while he was never resistant to change—especially in the local music scene—he clung tightly to "Old Hawai'i" and its customs and traditions. But Hawai'i was about to change forever.

In the lives of the Andersons there came a sort of intermezzo, a period of contentment that seemed to be endless. In retrospect, it was also a time of waiting and watching while the world underwent changes.

After taking temporary lodgings in Mānoa, the Anderson clan moved into a house on the beach at Waikīkī. The new home, at 2987 Kalākaua Avenue, belonged to Peggy's brother, Dad Center, who created the Outrigger Canoe Club's swim team and worked with swimming greats Duke Kahanamoku, James Lovett, Olga Clar, Buddy Crabbe, and Buster Crabbe. Center also coached the U.S. Olympic swim team in 1920. A renowned waterman, Dad Center was the first coach to use canoeing as a conditioning sport for swimmers. He and Duke Kahanamoku are credited with one of "the greatest rides of modern times" for when they surfed from Castle Point to Waikīkī Beach on thirty-foot swells born of an earthquake in Japan. Dad Center was as generous as he was capable: the home in Waikīkī had been willed to him by his mother, but it was far more house than he needed. With characteristic magnanimity he turned it over to the Andersons.

The house was in a wonderful location. Just beyond it there was a seawall, and beyond that were the beach and the sea. The Anderson children took to the water as if they all had gills, and they spent many days surfing off Diamond Head at prime surfing spots in one of the world's most picturesque settings. "Many of our friends brought their surfboards to our house and stacked them up against the house," Allen remembers. "We called ourselves The Waikīkī Athletic Club. During the week most of the outsiders didn't show, but on the weekends the place was crawling with them. Mother treated them like her own, often putting out large platters of rice and chop suey."

It was during this period that Alex wrote his most commercially successful song. He remembered the song's inspiration to an interviewer:

I was at a party, a private party, and in those days you could hire a quintet for maybe $50 for the evening, something very reasonable. Many people had music for their parties. This one evening we were at somebody's house . . . it was quite a good-sized party and people were seated around in a circle, and in the center of the room a hula girl was dancing. Out on the fringe a dozen or so of us men were standing, just listening. The guy next to me suddenly said, "Aren't her hands lovely?" Just like that, it struck him. She was very graceful, and he said, "Aren't her hands lovely?" And right away it hit me. I thought, there, that's the key to a good hula, and right away I started thinking about a song.

That one took three or four months. I didn't work on it constantly. See, I'd have ideas and put them on paper, then I'd think of something else and make a change, work it over again. During that time I was on a cruise down in New Zealand. There were six of us on a yacht, cruising around New Zealand waters and the lines in the song about "graceful as the birds in motion . . . gliding like the gulls o'er the ocean" came to me from that. Every day we had these gulls in back of the boat and that put that in my mind.

The resulting song, "Lovely Hula Hands," was an instant hit. It was both melodic and rich in its hula movements, so it was as often danced as it was sung: "Telling of the rain in the valley, and the swirling winds on the Pali, / lovely hula hands, *kou lima nani ē*."

Alex occasionally used Hawaiian words or phrases in his music, but he never attempted to write a song with full Hawaiian lyrics. His music was often referred to as *hapa haole*, which is defined in a Hawaiian dictionary by Mary Kawena Pukui and Samuel H. Elbert as part white, part Hawaiian. Pukui and Elbert explain that a *mele* (song) *hapa haole* is a Hawaiian type of song with English words and perhaps a few Hawaiian words. Alex made the phrase timeless as far as music is concerned. It is probable that many of the dancers who did the hula to this song never knew that *kou lima nani ē* means "your pretty fingers."

"Lovely Hula Hands" was recorded by more artists than any other Anderson tune, and while Alex was grateful for the royalties, the song was never his favorite. His favorite remained "Haole Hula," which expressed his love for the islands, although to one interviewer he claimed that "White Ginger Blossoms" was his favorite.

It seemed the songs were now tumbling out. "Two Shadows on the Sand," written with Norman Burlingame, was followed by "Blue Lei," with Milton Beamer, and then one of the most haunting of his melodies, "I Will Remember You," produced in 1941 with Carter Nott. The lyrics to "I Will Remember You" spoke of a profound loneliness:

> When the winds of winter come crying through the darkness
> Your lovely voice will come to me
> Even though in spirit across a mighty ocean
> Crying, Hawai'i Nei.

The words were prophetic of the changes that were about to explode upon Hawai'i, bringing separation and the heartache of being apart:

> I will remember you,
> 'Till the spring of another year,
> 'Till I hold you close again, I will remember you.

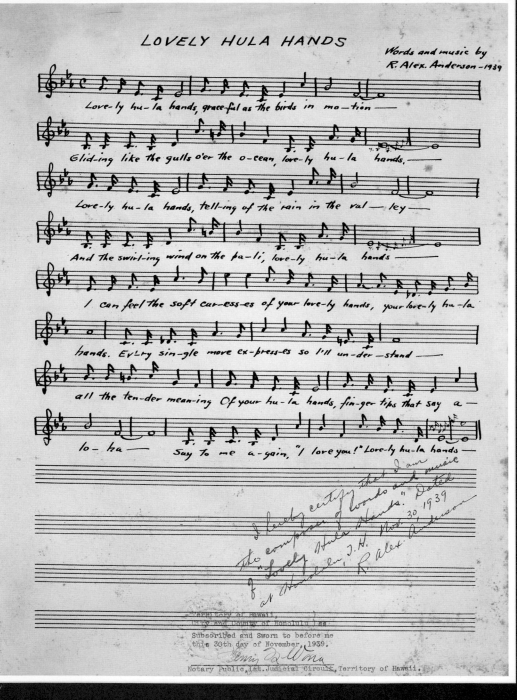

Alex's own musical score for Lovely Hula Hands bore his certification that it was, indeed, his creation. The year was 1939, the song is still popular.

I WILL REMEMBER YOU

Words and Music by R. Alex Anderson
and
Carter Nott

INTRODUCED BY
GIGGIE ROYSE
AND HIS ALEXANDER YOUNG

PUBLISHED BY
ANDERSON SONGS
HONOLULU ~ HAWAII

This was one of Alex's greatest hits, and is still heard. In 1941 this sheet music sold for fifty cents a copy, which included wrapping and mailing.

Lovely Hula Hands

Words and Music by
R. ALEX. ANDERSON
ASCAP

FEATURED BY
AGGIE AULD

PUBLISHED BY
ANDERSON SONGS • HONOLULU HAWAII

Lovely Hula Hands was one of Alex's best-known melodies, a tune that lingered in his head for a time before he finally put it down on paper.

LOVELY HULA HANDS

Words & Music by
R. ALEX. ANDERSON
A.S.C.A.P.

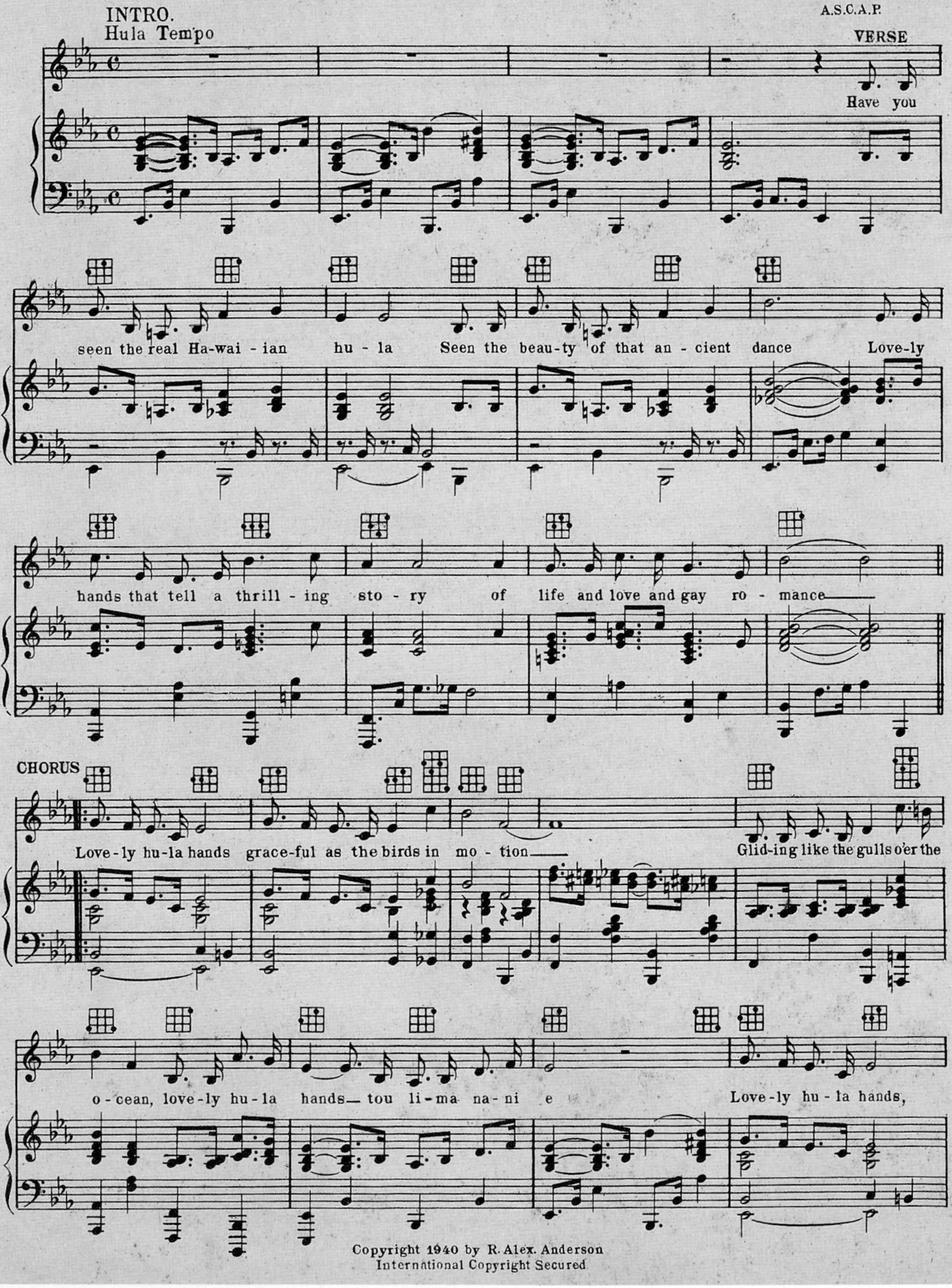

telling of the rain in the val-ley___ And the swirl-ing wind on the pa-li love-ly hu-la

hands_tou li-ma na-ni e___ I can feel the soft ca-ress-es of your love-ly hands, your love-ly hu-la

hands___ Ev'-ry lit-tle move ex-press-es so I'll un-der-stand all the ten-der mean-ing

Of your hu-la hands, fin-ger tips that say, "A - lo - ha"___ Say to me a-gain,"I

love you!" LOVE-LY HU-LA HANDS, tou li-ma na-ni e HANDS tou li-ma na-ni e

*She was grace and beauty personified, and Aggie Auld
was the first to dance Lovely Hula Hands. It has since*

CHAPTER 15

On December 7, 1941, Pam Anderson was up early, poking around in a tide pool along the reef. She was ten years old, and she enjoyed a child's uncomplicated pleasure in the colors in the water and the marine life in the pools on the balmy Sunday morning. When she raised her eyes from the tide pools and looked in the direction of Honolulu Harbor, she saw a freighter, and as she paused to watch it, an airplane suddenly appeared above the ship and curled into a dive, dropping something toward the freighter. A waterspout erupted alongside the ship. There was another plane overhead, and Pam could see the red ball of the sun insignia beneath the wings quite clearly. She turned and dashed for the house.

Alex was still sleeping, but Pam didn't hesitate to wake him up. Alex immediately turned on the radio and reached for the telephone to find that his worst fears were confirmed.

North of Oʻahu, a Japanese task force positioned itself for attack, and in the freshness of morning they hurled 360 aircraft against military installations on Oʻahu. The first wave deployed at 7:40 a.m., and the second wave came at 8:50, flying from the decks of the Japanese carriers. The Japanese had an armada of thirty-one ships that had stolen across the North Pacific to bring death and destruction to the military in Hawaiʻi—and, of course, to any civilians who got in the way.

The Anderson household came alive. From their vantage point in Waikīkī they had an excellent view of the action going on at Hickam Field, and they knew that all Oʻahu military installations were being hit.

Alex was a reserve police officer, one of a number of local business-men who had signed on out of a sense of duty. He and the others were called upon immediately. He left the house early that morning, and his family did not see him again for some forty-eight hours. When he came home they learned that he had been out on the highway directing traffic while the wounded were being brought up from Pearl Harbor to Tripler Army Hospital. Alex was shaken by what saw, but he stayed on duty until he was relieved.

That morning Governor Joseph B. Poindexter was told that Japanese troops might land on the island the next day, and that it was time for drastic action. Although the governor said it was the hardest thing he ever had to do, Hawai'i came swiftly under martial law. Among the civilian populace, there was considerable tension. A debate erupted over what should be done with the 160,000 Japanese living in Hawai'i. In California, Japanese and Japanese-Americans were being put in camps, and the fabric of Hawai'i's society was being torn, not to be fully mended until after the war.

In the Anderson household, the attack on Pearl Harbor and other military installations roused the boys to a sudden height of patriotism. "The blackout that night was pretty hairy," Allen recalls. "We had accumulated over the years quite an arsenal consisting of shotguns and rifles, with plenty of ammunition. So we sat up by twos watching the machine guns firing along the beach toward town. The Army had set up machine gun nests at intervals along the beach. The next day they strung barbed wire along the seawall, which made it pretty businesslike."

By the following March many business people were urged by the military to make the hard decision to send their families to the mainland. The idea of the Hawaiian Islands coming under attack again was enough to start a small exodus of woman and children to the West Coast.

Alex was unwilling to put Peggy and Pam and his youngest son, Allen, in a position of danger, so the three of them boarded a Pan American China Clipper for the seventeen-hour flight to San Francisco. Peggy found a place to rent in Palo Alto, to Allen's satisfaction—he didn't like San Francisco, where he had to wear shoes and had difficulty finding the sun between the buildings. The two older boys, Bob and Leith, were already aiming for wartime service, and Alex, now forty-seven, planned to maintain his reserve police status and look out for the family's interests in Hawai'i during the separation.

Nonessential civilians had been urged to leave the islands for the best of reasons—they would free up essential resources. Still, many who left were criticized by remaining residents who failed to realize that even military dependents had been ordered to leave. Meanwhile, Hawai'i went on the defensive, putting trenches, barbed wire, and pillboxes in place in preparation for a new Japanese attack or even an invasion.

Such an occurrence was not only possible, it was part of Japan's strategic thinking. Geographer Fusazo Motogawa wrote in April 1942 that "in order to bring America to defeat, Japan will be thinking about options for achieving war aims: carrying out an invasion and occupation of Hawai'i, using Hawai'i as a base for striking the United States mainland, using Hawai'i as a pivot for consolidating control of the South Pacific, and using Hawai'i to interdict American military and commercial communications."

This never came about, of course, because the Japanese attack on the Pacific Fleet turned out to be a monumental failure. The Japanese task-force commander, Vice Admiral Chuichi Nagumo, hardly believed his good fortune in accomplishing a complete surprise attack on Pearl Harbor, and not knowing the whereabouts of the U.S. aircraft carriers with their deckloads of deadly aircraft, he ruled out a second attack. A second attack would have focused on the repair facilities, the fuel storage, and the submarine pens. But the cautious Nagumo felt he had gambled and won and was not going to gamble a second time.

The American submarines were soon at sea prowling for Japanese ships. Many of the sunken or damaged American ships were salvaged and repaired in the naval shipyard and were soon back in action with sufficient fuel to carry the war to the Japanese. Even after the Battle of Midway inflicted severe losses on the Japanese fleet—most historians agree it was the turning point of the war in the Pacific—Japanese propagandists continued to tell the Japanese public that Hawai'i and Midway had been sensational victories and that Japan controlled the Central Pacific.

Meanwhile, every home in Hawai'i was required to construct some sort of shelter against additional attacks. Lei makers were put to work making camouflage nets, and each family was told to assemble an "evacuation kit." Blackouts were enforced by blackout wardens patrolling the neighborhoods. The curfew was also strictly enforced, which brought most nighttime activities to a halt. Alex, serving as a reserve police officer, was issued passes for specific times and places. One such pass dated February 19, 1942, read: "Bearer, Mr. R. A. Anderson, residing at 2987 Kalākaua Avenue, has been granted permission to travel during blackout hours only for the purpose of going to and from Red Hill." It inspired one of Alex's more forgettable, but certainly topical, songs—"She's a Knockout in a Blackout."

A famous incident that occurred during the Japanese attack led to another song. A Japanese pilot's plane was hit, forcing him to land on the privately owned island of Ni'ihau, which was occupied almost entirely by Hawaiians. The pilot landed safely and began to terrorize the tiny island. At one point he decided to shoot a Hawaiian named Benehakaka Kanahele and his wife, but the fifty-one-year-old Kanahele rushed the pilot. The Japanese pilot shot Kanahele three times in the stomach, but Kanahele never stumbled; he picked up the pilot and brained him against a stone wall.

Alex loved that story, and he translated it into a song called "They Couldn't Take Ni'ihau Nohow":

So they couldn't take Ni'ihau nohow, when big Kanahele said "pau."
He made a grand slam for his Uncle Sam, and
They couldn't take Ni'ihau nohow.

The song was added, in march tempo, to the repertoire of the 264th U.S. Army Band. And it was not overlooked by the brass: on November 14, 1944, currency from the ill-fated Japanese pilot's pocket was sent to Alex as a souvenir. The sender was Admiral Chester W. Nimitz.

During the time that his family was on the mainland, Alex had plenty of time to look back over what certainly was beginning to seem to have been a more peaceful time and a more gracious era. He thought of the home at 2978 Pacific Heights Road, with its 3.5 acres of land overlooking beautiful Nu'uanu Valley, where two of his four children were born. He remembered the Japanese couple, Naka and Hideko, who worked for the family, and the white leghorn chickens they raised, and the time the family found out that they had twenty-two fox terriers. He remembered Sunday mornings and Sunday School at Saint Andrews Cathedral, which was always followed by a trip to his mother's house at Ke'eaumoku and Nehoa streets for a Sunday type of meal—he always brought the chicken.

And he remembered his father, the big man with the walrus mustache who was always dressed in white suit and bow tie, fashionably carrying a cane. He thought of his father playing the organ and piano and he thought of his gentle mother and her love of music. He also thought about his immediate family who were now so far away.

Perhaps the happiest times for the family had taken place at Dad Center's house on Kalākaua Avenue. The children became excellent swimmers, canoeists, and board surfers under Dad Center's expert tutelage. When

THEY COULDN'T TAKE NIIHAU NOHOW

Words and Music by
R. ALEX ANDERSON

Composed by
R. ALEX ANDERSON

MILLER MUSIC, INC.
1619 BROADWAY · NEW YORK

On the 'forbidden' island of Ni'ihau a Japanese pilot, downed in the Pearl Harbor attack, terrorized the island until a big Hawaiian killed him. Alex translated the story to music,

July 21 1943

Dear Mr. Anderson:

Many thanks to you for your letter of
July 17, and for the photostatic copy of the
music of one of your recent songs which I have
heard and liked very much.

With kindest regards and best wishes.

Sincerely yours,

C. W. NIMITZ

Mr. R. A. Anderson,
Post Office Box 2271,
Honolulu, Hawaii.

and later Admiral Chester W. Nimitz (inset) sent Alex some currency

each child turned sixteen, Dad gave them junior memberships to the Outrigger Canoe Club. Leith and Pam, especially, became top-ranked surfers. Pam, in fact, was the top woman surfer at the Outrigger and the reigning women's canoe steersman. Leith was the club's number one Hobie-cat sailor, and Bob was the top men's canoe steersman. Allen was a club member for years and a "water rat" like the others.

Sports played a large part in their family life. When the children were not in the water they were on it, sailing at the Pearl Harbor Yacht Club. Alex had taught all the children to sail, and he also got them started in tennis and golf. For Alex, sports were a joy, but golf was a passion. He had joined Harold Castle, Arthur Rice, and Kelly Henshaw in putting up three thousand dollars each to build a small clubhouse and the first nine holes of what became the Mid-Pac Country Club, with an eighteen-hole championship course. He was a founding member of the Wai'alae Country Club, which became his "home course" in later years, and he was an early member of the O'ahu Country Club. He eventually became an honorary life member of all three clubs. He was a six-handicap golfer and taught Pam so well that she became the Wai'alae Club Champion several times, and she was always high in the state's ranking of women golfers.

As he reminisced, Alex felt that his family had known true happiness, and he was happy with the way his children had turned out. Bob, later, had this evaluation of the children's upbringing:

> Both Mother and Dad set examples of very high standards of moral and personal behavior and character, throughout our lives. I think if there were one overriding contribution that their examples and standards set, and made their lasting impressions on us, it was their total honesty and encouragement always to do the right and kind thing. Mother was our caretaker and sternest disciplinarian. Dad was a lot easier, but in the early years we didn't "know" him nearly as well as Mother; easy to understand in looking back—Mother was always with us; Dad was working and involved in many things outside the family activities. Not to say he wasn't interested, because he often pried himself loose to come to a track meet or a tennis match, etc. But Mom was with us a greater part of the time. Later in life, it evened out.

Alex's interests went far beyond his own pleasures. In the twenties and thirties he had become increasingly community oriented and offered his services generously. He was an early member of the Honolulu Chamber of Commerce, the Honolulu Rotary Club (where he was to become district governor of the Rotary), the Commercial Club (a business luncheon club), the Pacific Club, and others. "My recollection about Dad's personal nature and actions through all of the many civic involvements and activities of his lifetime," Bob Anderson recalled, "was that he did things and gave of his time freely but always quietly, never looking for credit or acclaim. Whether it was serving on boards of directors or organizing a music company or activity, he did it with enthusiasm and dedication but always low-key . . .one of the last people that you might think would have the awesome list of credits toward personal giving that summarized his life."

Alex was a founding member of one of his favorite organizations, the Order of Daedalians, which was a military pilot's organization. He also was a founding member of the "QB"—the Quiet Birdmen's organization for both civilian and military pilots. A few of his fellow members saw Alex as the prime mover in airport construction when he served as chairman of the Territorial Aeronautics Commission. In that capacity he had objected to the proposed construction of an airport on the leeward shore of Moloka'i and fought for its relocation to a safer site farther inland.

Throughout all of this activity, Peggy had not been idle. She continued with her voice lessons after leaving Madame Melba, and she was also an active member of the Honolulu Morning Music Club, the Outdoor Circle, the Junior League, and the Daughters of Hawai'i. With Alex's help, she succeeded in bringing to Hawai'i Madame Melba's famous music director, Fritz Hart, to be conductor of the Honolulu Symphony. It was the first real step toward establishing the symphony as a viable organization.

Peggy and Pam were gone about eighteen months, and the separation was a particularly painful time for a family that had been so close. Perhaps that pain of separation was what Alex had in mind when he wrote, in 1943, a song called "No Tears":

No tears shall dim your lovely eyes,
Only a smile to bless our last good-byes.
No tears shall cloud that dearest face,
Lips that are smiling will meet in fond embrace.

Being separated from his family for a time in World War II
led Alex to write No Tears, which sang that "no distance nor time
can ever come between us."

NO TEARS

Words and Music by
R. ALEX ANDERSON

3

Our love has been so per - fect, hal - lowed by your sun - ny smile. Tho' we face sad sep - a - ra - tion, Re - mem - ber, it's just for a while.

CHAPTER 16

When Alex's family got back to Hawai'i, they returned to a new home. The family had hardly gotten off to the mainland when Dad Center had decided to get married, which meant he would be needing the house on Kalākaua Avenue. Alex looked around, and with the help of a realtor friend he found a place that charmed him at once. It was at 2954 Mākālei Place, in a superb location on the front side of Diamond Head, a sunswept, rambling Mediterranean-style home with several levels and plenty of bedrooms. It was close enough to the water, and the price was right. Alex looked forward to showing it off to his family when they all returned. He meant it to be their final and permanent home, which is what it became.

Peggy and Pam came home directly from California, but the boys took a more circuitous route. After the war ended, Bob was separated at Camp Beale, California, in October 1945. He promptly bought a Plymouth coupe and headed east with the intention of finding his brothers. Finding Allen was no problem—he picked him up at Truax Field in Madison, Wisconsin, and the two headed up to Wallingford, Connecticut, to visit Choate, the prep school they had attended. Then the brothers drove to Norfolk, Virginia, where Ensign Leith Anderson was continuing to train in carrier landings. Bob and Allen arrived after lunch, only to learn that just that morning Leith and two flying buddies had left by car for California. Bob and Allen headed back west, driving virtually nonstop across the country. Bad luck dogged them in Nevada; in Lovelock the Plymouth threw a rod, and they were detained for a full week while they waited for two mechanics to rebuild the engine. Finally they were able to drive on to San Francisco. In San Francisco, Bob and Allen learned that they could catch a

The home on Mākālei Place was a sunswept, Mediterranean-type villa, and always full of the sound of music.

ride home on a Navy hospital ship, the USS *Repose*. Allen remembered the crossing as slow; Bob said it was a rough voyage. They arrived in Honolulu in early December to find that Leith had beaten them home by one week.

The house at Mākālei Place—which was actually a villa sitting on a Hawaiian hillside—rang with the festivities of homecoming. Not one to pass up such a marvelous opportunity for a party, Alex made sure the family had a memorable homecoming fete. Bob, especially, would remember the party well, for at the celebration he met the woman he was to marry.

Alex quickly put the malaise of the war behind him. When the Royal Hawaiian Hotel was refurbished and opened again—after serving as a military rest and recreation site during the war—Alex felt stirred enough to write a song that transcended the hotel opening and expressed his feelings in general; he called it "It's Time to Play Again." In spite of his already burgeoning schedule, he still had time to maintain an interest in photography and carpentry. He also became a part of the Hawai'i Aeronautics Commission, serving from May 24, 1947, to May 21, 1953. And he did not neglect his work—by 1952 he was vice president and assistant manager of Von Hamm-Young. Another activity that kept him busy in 1953 was serving as chairman of the Red Cross's annual fund drive.

Still his songs poured forth like water from a deep well. In 1948, with Jack Owens, he wrote the rich, melodic "I'll Weave a Lei of Stars for You": "The moon is green with jealousy, and all the planets too, / And when you wear my lei of stars the fairest one is you."

A year later Alex was in his office at Von Hamm-Young when his secretary—a woman from the mainland—mentioned that she had never heard a good Hawaiian Christmas song. "I hadn't either," Alex recalled, "so I wrote one." The resulting song was played and sung for years afterwards and showed all signs of becoming a classic. "It was an overnight job," Alex said. Called "Mele Kalikimaka" ("Merry Christmas"), it was destined to become a part of all future Christmases in the islands:

Mele Kalikimaka is the thing to say
On a bright Hawaiian Christmas Day.
That's the Island greeting that we send to you
From the land where palm trees sway.

Scottish writer Iain Finlayson has noted that "the traditional Scots sense of humor is subtle, sharp, pithy and dry." Add to that the island influence, which can at times be ribald or sly, and the result was that Alex had no hesitation in writing songs that reflected his sense of fun. One example is a song that was copyrighted in 1953. Written with Peter Lee Zoellner and Fred T. Smith, it was called "Mu'umu'u Māmā":

Mu'umu'u Māmā, tell me what I've got to do
To get a look at you. The missionaries did it,
They went and hid it, underneath a big mu'umu'u.

Another song from this period, "Holiday Hula," reflected the local approach to celebration:

Holiday hula, I'm in the mood for
Paper hats, whistles and noise,
From your singing lips to your swinging hips
Tell the story of holiday joys.

In the immediate postwar years there were plenty of celebrations, and Alex and Peggy entertained many celebrities who came to Hawai'i— national and international performers, top businessmen who had dealings with Von Hamm-Young, and military people, who were always appreciative of the fact that Alex was a strong supporter of the military over the years. When Alex and Peggy celebrated their twenty-fifth wedding anniversary on November 14, 1944, Admirals Chester W. Nimitz and William

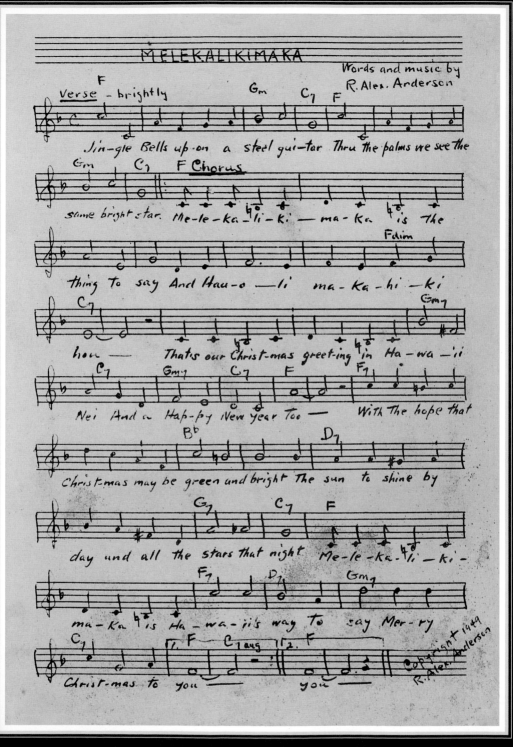

One of Alex's most popular melodies came when a friend asked why there were no songs about Christmas in Hawai'i.

Another song that endured, Mele Kalikimaka. It was given wide popularity when it was recorded by Bing Crosby and the Andrew Sisters.

Hawaii's Way of Saying "Merry Christmas!"

MELE KALIKIMAKA

(pronounced "Me-Lee Ka-Lee-Ki-Ma-Ka")

Key of F (B-D)

Words and Music by
R. ALEX. ANDERSON

Verse: Jin-gle bells up-on a steel gui-tar, Through the palms we see the same bright star.

Chorus: ME-LE KA-LI-KI-MA-KA is the thing to say,____ On a bright Ha-wai-ian Christ-mas day,____ That's the Is-land

L 870-2

Copyright MCMXLIX by Pickwick Music Corporation, New York, N. Y.
Copyright 1950 by **PICKWICK MUSIC CORPORATION**, RKO Bldg., Radio City, New York, N. Y.

Roy Crane was a famous artist when he was entertained by Peggy and Alex, and from that memorable evening came a riotous cartoon by Crane.

H. "Bull" Halsey were out in the courtyard of the Mākālei Place home, among other military brass. Irving Berlin stopped by on another occasion to sit in the Anderson's living room and play a few tunes, including some written by Alex. "We're tuneful people," he told Alex. Bob Hope and Jack Benny were there. On one memorable occasion, Edgar Bergen, the ventriloquist par excellence, sat both his companions, Charlie McCarthy and Mortimer Snerd, out on the reef and called to them, and all around him an appreciative audience swore the two dummies called back. Andy Williams was a guest at one courtyard party, and Bill Dana, Dick Powell, Cole Porter, and Martin Denny also showed up.

The parties were almost always at the home, and they were usually catered. "There was a group of catering ladies—the same ones everybody knew—and a bartender," Pam remembers. "The parties were always happy ones, ending with mother and dad singing, and occasionally there would be other music groups there. People went home at a decent hour, people didn't carry on late in those days." Often the parties were relatively small, but Pam remembers one gathering of some two hundred people.

Entertaining with Aloha...

With Arthur Godfrey, it wasn't all work, and he, Alex and Peggy found time to enjoy themselves during Godfrey's visits to Hawai'i.

Alex and Peggy and an unidentified couple with, in the center, singer Kay Starr.

A crewmember of the Matson liner *Lurline* snapped this photo of Peggy and Alex entertaining aboard the ship.

The home built by the Anderson family in the Wai'anae Range was a "getaway"
place for the Anderson clan and they equipped it with everything but a telephone.

Another happy memory the family shared was the building of a
"mountain home" on Campbell Estate land in the Wai'anae mountains
range, at a place called Pālehua (Hawaiian for an enclosure of the lehua
flower). The year was 1949, and a family friend, Herbert Von Holt, was
then head of Campbell Estate. There were some ten parcels of land at
Pālehua that the estate was willing to lease, and Von Holt agreed that
Alex could lease one of the acre-and-a-half parcels. There was power on
the site, and Alex and his brood set about building a home. They began by
buying railroad ties from the defunct O. R. and L. Railroad that ran from
Iwilei, near downtown Honolulu, out to the leeward sugarcane fields. The
ties were creosoted and looked as if they might last forever; Alex got them
for a dollar a tie. Making it a family affair, Alex borrowed a truck from the
Von Hamm-Young company and enlisted the rest of the family to help
haul the ties up the mountain. "It took many, many trips," Pam remembers.

Alex and Peggy built a work shack at the site, where Peggy pushed the ties through to Alex's electric saw and he grooved them. Everyone then pitched in to help construct the house that Alex designed. He had envisioned a home of fourteen to fifteen thousand square feet that would take advantage of the fabulous view. Not until it came time to put in the windows, the roof, and the last part of the flooring did they call in professional carpenters to help finish off the home.

The house was striking enough to be featured in Sunset Magazine. It was a home with a large plate-glass window that afforded a view all the way from the Waiʻanae Range to Diamond Head on one side and Waiʻanae down into Mākaha Valley on the other. Water on the site was provided by a catchment tank found in ʻAiea, which was disassembled, driven up to Pālehua, and put back together by the children. Alex put a liner in it, and it became their permanent water supply. They chose not to have a telephone.

The mountain home became a weekend refuge for Alex and Peggy and an occasional guest, such as Peter Lawford. The children used it as well. The family held on to the house for years, and Pam, who eventually went into real estate, sold it in the eighties.

If the mountain home was a getaway place, it wasn't the only one. Alex and Peggy, now in their middle years, were enjoying life and especially enjoying travel. Both were in excellent health, and they had financial security since the Von Hamm-Young Company was doing very well. In fact, the company provided a reason to travel. Alex used his presence abroad to call on representatives of his company's suppliers, the firms from whom Von Hamm-Young imported their products. One such firm was General Motors, and each time that the Andersons turned up in Europe, GM provided a car

Alex enjoyed his rapport with a giant in the building business — industrialist Henry J. Kaiser.

and a driver, a Frenchman named André who transported them wherever they wanted to go. On one of these trips, Alex and Peggy were accompanied by Paul and Ruth Winslow; on another Pam went along and played golf with Alex in Scotland and in Germany's Black Forest. Alex especially enjoyed Scotland, and when he played the course at Turnberry memories of his old Forty Squadron were close and strong.

Peggy, who never had to work after marrying Alex, stayed busy with household chores, frequent entertaining, and with her interests in the Junior League, the Daughters of Hawai'i, the Garden Club, and other organizations. It was an upbeat time for the Andersons and for Hawai'i, a time when tourism was growing into a lucrative business, and the ripple effect was felt throughout the economy. It was a time when there was talk of statehood in the air, and Alex strongly supported that idea, feeling that statehood would be beneficial to the islands.

Alex had never forgotten the people who helped him escape in World War I—the Belgian families who were instrumental in his survival. Since the war he had kept in touch with them at least once a year, often at Christmas. As the years passed it became obvious to Alex that those families were not going to visit Hawai'i, so Alex decided to visit them. He would go back to Belgium.

Three times over a period of ten years Alex made the journey back to Brussels to see the Van den Corput and Hus families, each time staying for a week or so. It had been thirty-five years since his escape, and, as Peggy put it,

> We found and were with the older generation, who have since passed on. Now we are communicating with their grown children. Every Christmas the beautiful letters come . . . and during the year when I have a birthday and Andy has one . . . they write us, and on our anniversary, the same way. The younger generation are now communicating with us. They love him dearly because he came from the middle of the Pacific and thought enough of them to go back and find them. And you can't believe it but our grandchildren have been entertained in the homes of the younger generation because their children are the same age as our grandchildren who have been in college in Switzerland. Isn't it wonderful?

During one of the trips back, Pam said, Madame Van den Corput's health was failing rapidly. She held on long enough to see Alex, Peggy, and Pam, and she died two days after they visited her.

Other travels did not hold the same significance, but they were pleasant. Alex and Peggy visited Australia and New Zealand, and they drove across the United States twice. Alex maintained a certain international awareness, and while he had no outspoken opinion on the Korean War, he was a staunch backer of the idea that the United States had a responsibility concomitant with its strength, that the nation should always be involved in international affairs. He realized that the military was one arm of international policy, and he remained a supporter.

It was a time when Alex knew that he was in the prime of life and that life was, indeed, good. Those who knew him well knew that he had no hesitation in acknowledging that he was very grateful for what he felt God had given him.

Alex was aviator, songwriter — and businessman. Normally clad in an aloha shirt, he could dress for business affairs when need be.

Lovely Hula Hands

Words and Music by
R. ALEX ANDERSON

Featured by
RAY KINNEY
and his Hawaiian Musical Ambassadors

MILLER MUSIC, INC.

A good song goes on and on.
Lovely Hula Hands is timeless,
and was performed often by
the well-known local
entertainer, Ray Kinney.

Lovely Hula Hands was so popular it became
an aloha shirt, and not surprisingly,
a shirt that Alex wore often.

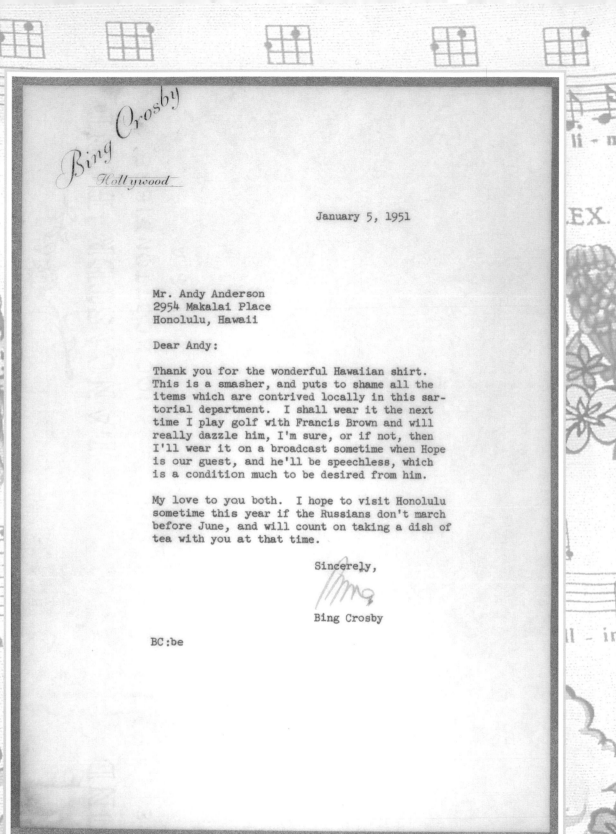

Bing Crosby

Hollywood

January 5, 1951

Mr. Andy Anderson
2954 Makalai Place
Honolulu, Hawaii

Dear Andy:

Thank you for the wonderful Hawaiian shirt.
This is a smasher, and puts to shame all the
items which are contrived locally in this sar-
torial department. I shall wear it the next
time I play golf with Francis Brown and will
really dazzle him, I'm sure, or if not, then
I'll wear it on a broadcast sometime when Hope
is our guest, and he'll be speechless, which
is a condition much to be desired from him.

My love to you both. I hope to visit Honolulu
sometime this year if the Russians don't march
before June, and will count on taking a dish of
tea with you at that time.

Sincerely,

Bing Crosby

BC:be

*Bing Crosby remained a good friend, and managed his own note
of whimsy in this letter to Alex.*

CHAPTER *17*

Some called it the "fearful fifties," some the "fretful fifties," and perhaps there were good reasons for both names. The world was changing rapidly with such events as the Korean War, the creation of fallout shelters in the face of a nuclear threat, Joseph McCarthy and the witch hunts, the Mau Mau uprising in Kenya, China's invasion of Tibet, and Castro ousting Batista and beginning a Communist regime on America's doorstep.

In Hawai'i the population stood at about a half million. Japanese, Koreans, and Samoans were becoming eligible for U.S. citizenship, and the islands were rolling down a path that would lead to statehood in 1959, a move local people approved by a ratio of seventeen to one.

Alex's music was played all over the world now, and it continued to be the defining sound that sang "Hawai'i" to a world newly interested in these islands, which were seen as remote and romantic. At home Alex's talents were now long recognized and often put to use. In 1955 he wrote "Fellowship of the Rotary" for the Honolulu Rotary Club, where he had become a fixture. He wrote an original song for the "Smile Girl" contest and a song for the July 22, 1955, presentation dinner of the Trans-Pacific Yacht Race. It was probably as close to doggerel as he ever got:

> On the 4th of July we hoisted sail,
> To cross the blue Pacific.
> The wind was fresh to near a gale
> And this made the race terrific.

This went on for several stanzas in which he recognized the winning ships, the female sailors, the sailors from the Orient and from Down Under, and even the one ship that hadn't made it in time for the dinner.

A year later he wrote two new songs for the Junior League Ball, and the year after that he wrote "Royal Hawaiian" to celebrate the thirtieth birthday of that storied old hotel on the beach at Waikīkī. It came as no real surprise that he was elected "Father of the Year" from the field of entertainment and was so honored at the Lincoln Day dinner in 1958. That year the American Legion gave him a certificate for twenty-five continuous years of membership.

Other music was surfacing from his fertile brain: "Aloha Malihini," which he wrote with Don McDiarmid; and "Hula Rock," in which he acknowledged the new music:

> Then all at once there came a change,
> Something different, something strange.
> To the little grass skirts in the little grass shacks
> Rock and Roll was with 'em.

In "Coral Reefs" he returned to the more traditional style that he was most comfortable with, and he accompanied it with "Just an Orchid from Hawai'i" and a string of others. It was a very productive period—between 1950–60 he copyrighted twenty-one songs and wrote even more than that. In 1958 he wrote original music to honor both the Narcissus Queen and the Cherry Blossom Queen, paying gracious tribute to both. The lyrics of "Narcissus Queen" described a "gentle Oriental maid, wearing gold and precious jade," while the fair damsel of the Cherry Blossom fete was "dainty and shy . . . a true butterfly of old Japan." With the coming of statehood Alex teamed up with Peter Lee Zoellner and Fred T. Smith to produce a song that was unabashed in its opinion that America was far better off for adding Hawai'i to its roster of states. The writers called it "Hawai'i U.S.A.":

> Hawai'i, the pride of the U.S.A.
> The shining star of the nation,
> The pearl of the seven seas,
> The fairest land in creation.

Late in the decade, Alex suffered one of his few setbacks. A poster from 1958 that calls him "R. Alexander Alika Anderson" shows Alex as a

Republican candidate for representative from the sixteenth district. His GOP opponents were John De Mello, Henry Haina, George Ing, and Eddie Yamasaki. Alex got the most votes for his party, and all but De Mello moved on to the general election. In the general election the GOP candidates ran into the same Democratic blitzkrieg that had swept the Republicans out of power in 1954. The Democratic side was headed by a man destined to spend the rest of his life in politics, Spark M. Matsunaga. Matsunaga headed up a field that included Tadao Beppu, Hiroshi Kato, and Walter Heen. It was a Democratic sweep, with 88 percent of eligible voters turning out to elect the Democrats and Matsunaga getting the most votes.

But Alex ran a good, strong campaign, and his family was behind the effort. A newspaper photo from that time shows Peggy and Pam handing out sheet music with political notes on them. Another photo shows Alex with the whole brood. His campaign poster did not rely solely on his musical accomplishments. It listed his twenty years with the Hawaiʻi Visitors Bureau, eight years with the Hawaiʻi Aeronautics Commission (four of them as chairman), five years as president of the Honolulu Symphony Society, twenty years as a trustee of Lēʻahi Hospital, four years as director of the Red Cross, and current presidency of the Downtown Improvement Association. When it was all over Alex received a letter from Art Woolaway, GOP committeeman for the territory. "Although you did not win," Woolaway wrote to Alex, "your participation and efforts, so admirably demonstrated, more than added to the successes we achieved."

Old favorites continued to stay around. Lawrence Welk wrote to Alex on October 14, 1959, saying that he'd had the opportunity to include two Anderson songs, "Lovely Hula Hands" and "The Cockeyed Mayor of Kaunakakai," on his show. At around the same time, Andy Williams forwarded an album and a letter, saying in part, "I'm sending you a new album of Hawaiian songs of which 'I'll Weave a Lei of Stars for You' is my favorite. It's the prettiest one in the album. Thank you for writing it." Equally gratifying were the royalty checks that came regularly from all over the world. Alex was so encouraged by them that he once told a friend that if he could start all over, he might just forget about being a businessman and focus on the music; that he could have perhaps supported himself and his family solely on the income from his songs.

The decade of the 1960s did nothing to slow down Alex's productivity, despite the changes that came to Von Hamm-Young and demanded his attention. Once again he copyrighted twenty-one songs in a ten-year

Andy Williams

September 11, 1959

Dear Alex:

I am sending you the new album of Hawaiian songs
of which, " I'll Weave A Lei Of Stars For You " is
my favorite. It is the prettiest one in the album,
and I want to thank you for writing it. I hope you
like it too.

Please give my best to Jane and Bob and Mrs. Anderson.
Hope to see you soon.

Best,

Andy

Andy

AW/n

Mr. Alex Anderson
2954 Makalei Place
Honolulu, Hawaii

*Andy Williams took the time to write to Alex about the song
he considered "prettiest one in the album."*

span, and once again some of them were written for special occasions. In 1964 he copyrighted "Old Kāhala" to celebrate the opening of the Kahala Hilton Hotel (now the Kahala Mandarin Oriental). Still sharing his *aloha* with the military, he wrote with Sybil Webber "The Air Force Deb" and "The Army Debutante Waltz."

Almost as swiftly as the songs went out, demands for his services—and not only as a songwriter—came in. He was appointed a member of the Army Advisory Committee in Hawai'i, he was chairman of the annual Easter Seal campaign of the O'ahu Tuberculosis and Health Association in 1964, and he was named to Cornell University's council.

In the early part of September 1962 Alex was one of a twenty-man group of Hawai'i business ands civic leaders to make an important European visit. Led by *Honolulu Star-Bulletin* editor William H. Ewing and including *Honolulu Advertiser* editor George Chaplin, the group spent ten days in Russia, talking and listening. The newsmen returned with long editorial pieces about relations between Russia and the U.S., but Alex decided to keep it light. He wrote a song that included the lyrics "She says Nyet . . . I say Da, / I don't get very far."

After Russia the group went on to Warsaw, where they began to split up. Peggy left Hawai'i to meet Alex in Dusseldorf, Germany, where the musical "Hawai'i Aloha" was being produced with Alex as one of the backers. Peggy was joined by Paul and Ruth Winslow. On their return, Alex and Peggy took the time to drive leisurely across the United States.

Honors and recognitions continued to pour in. Alex was elected a member of the Century Club, formed for the advancement of the Aloha Council of the Boy Scouts of America. He was named Hawai'i's native-born citizen of 1969. He was enrolled as a member of the Golden Chapter of his fraternity, Pi Kappa Alpha, in recognition of his membership of fifty years. At a Honolulu Chamber of Commerce luncheon, where fathers of the year were named from various fields, Alex was selected for the major honor, the community-wide father of the year. He received ongoing honors from the Rotary—he had been a member of the Honolulu Rotary for sixty-four years at this time, having served as president from 1935–36 and district governor from 1956–57.

As a songwriter, Alex knew he could deliver when called on to do so, but it never became a big ego factor for him. He could, in fact, poke gentle fun at his own accomplishments, in the manner of a man who is secure in his talent. Not above spoofing one of his biggest hit songs, Alex

CORNELL UNIVERSITY

PRESENTS TO

R. ALEXANDER ANDERSON

THIS CERTIFICATE IN GRATEFUL RECOGNITION OF

FIFTY YEARS

OF LOYALTY AND DEVOTION TO CORNELL

JUNE 1966

PRESIDENT

Alex was a 1916 graduate of Cornell, and never forgot his alma mater. He was a staunch supporter all his life.

smiled to himself over the popularity of "Lovely Hula Hands" and set about writing a song in 1968 called "Waste Time Watch the Hands":

> Waste time watch the hands, keep your eyes on other things,
> Like the way she sways and swings when she does the hula,
> Her style and her smile, while you see it on her lips,
> Don't forget to watch the hips, when she does the hula.

Now in his seventies but apparently ageless, Alex as always was fascinated by Hawai'i as a melting pot of races, and he felt that Hawai'i was an example to the world and a blueprint for racial equality for the rest of the United States. With J. A. Stebbins and Ed Kenney, he turned out "That's What America is All About":

> Our forefathers came here from Europe,
> From Asia and from the Philippines,
> Tahiti, Samoa, the Antipodes—
> So you tell me please, what does that do to me
> If I am a quarter of each one of these?
> If Columbia's the gem of the ocean,
> And Hawai'i the pearl of the seas,
> Then I'm here to shout, without any doubt
> That's what America is all about.

He continued to share his gifts. A note from Andre Kostelanetz dated December 29, 1964, thanked Alex for his recording of "White Ginger Blossoms," which, the noted conductor said, "I enjoyed immensely." On May 24, 1966, a letter came from Odette Gilbert, secretary to Princess Grace of Monaco: "Her Serene Highness Princess Grace has asked me to reply to your letter of April 26, 1966. Her Highness would like to thank you sincerely for your good wishes and kind thoughts, which were deeply appreciated. Her Highness enjoyed very much listening to the records as well." A letter came from First Lady Patricia Nixon telling Alex that his "warm and friendly note saying welcome to Hawai'i was deeply appreciated by all the family." A few months later, President Nixon followed up with a thank-you note saying that it was kind of Alex to remember them during their visit to Hawai'i and that he'd appreciated the album "Soft Green Seas." Marine Corps Lieutenant General Victor Krulak sent over a note thanking Alex and Peggy for "a good evening."

A letter from Admiral John S. McCain, Jr., commander in chief, Pacific, thanked Alex for what surely must have been one of Alex's most enjoyable outings. On an invitation from McCain, Alex went out on the aircraft carrier USS Hornet to watch an operation that no doubt seemed remarkable to a man who, in his youth, had flown what he considered to be an advanced aircraft. From the deck of the carrier on November 24, 1969, Alex and other guests watched as Apollo Twelve astronauts Charles Conrad, Richard Gordon, and Alan Bean splashed down in the Pacific. In a thoughtful letter, McCain thanked Alex for "participating in the welcoming ceremony for these stalwart and courageous men." Alex had now been present in and a part of an era of aviation that began with canvas-wrapped single-engine highly fragile aircraft and evolved to include lunar modules and rocket engines. This may have been the inspiration for his upbeat "Rock, Rock, Rocket to the Moon":

> They blasted off upon a July morning,
> Kept their rocket on the beam;
> Far ahead the lunar day was dawning,
> They were weightless, and it was just like a dream.

Another military occasion warmed Alex's heart—and corrected an old oversight. At Pacific Air Forces headquarters, Hickam Air Force Base, on October 28, 1964, Alex stood alongside Lieutenant General Sam

Maddux, Jr., Vice Commander in Chief of Pacific Air Forces, and listened as a citation was read. Alex's thoughts went back to his stricken aircraft, his wounds, his imprisonment, and his escape. He remembered how, after he reached his own lines, the rapid winding down of the war and his swift return to the United States had meant a minimum of paperwork and probably a good many oversights. He listened to the citation noting his wounds, and then, forty-six years after he was wounded, Alex stood at attention as Maddux reached over and presented him with the Purple Heart medal.

Andre Kostelanetz

December 29th,
1 9 6 4

Mr. and Mrs. R. Alex Anderson
5954 Makalei Place
Honolulu, Hawaii

Dear Peggy and Andy

Your record "White Ginger Blossoms" just arrived and we enjoyed it enormously. You have composed very beautiful music and the record came out extremely well. Until we see you again, it will be our link to you and your beautiful island.

Sara Gene joins me in wishing you a very Happy New Year.

Sincerely yours,

With aloha

Andre —

10 Gracie Square
New York,
New York 10028

The Maestro dropped a personal note to Peggy and Alex (often called Andy — he answered to both) praising Alex's music.

COMMANDER IN CHIEF PACIFIC

5 December 1969

Dear Mr. Anderson,

I am most appreciative of the fine album, "White Ginger Blossoms," you so thoughtfully sent me. Your Hawaiian songs have brought me many wonderful hours of listening pleasure, and I shall treasure this album. Your renowned songs are among my most favorite.

It was indeed an honor and pleasure for me to have been on board the USS HORNET for the Apollo 12 recovery operations. It was unquestionably one of my most memorable experiences.

Thank you for participating in the welcoming ceremonies for these three stalwart and courageous men.

With renewed thanks for your generosity and warm regards,

Sincerely,

JOHN S. McCAIN, Jr.
Admiral, U. S. Navy

Mr. R. Alexander Anderson
2954 Makalei Place
Honolulu, Hawaii 96815

THE WHITE HOUSE
WASHINGTON

September 12, 1972

PERSONAL

Dear Mr. Anderson:

It was particularly kind of you to remember Mrs. Nixon and me so thoughtfully during our recent visit to Hawaii. Dr. Tkach has given us the inscribed copies of your album, "Soft Green Seas," and your accompanying song book, and we want you to know how much we appreciate this generous expression of friendship and goodwill.

With our very best wishes,

Sincerely,

Richard Nixon

Mr. R. Alex Anderson
2954 Makalei Place
Honolulu, Hawaii 96815

DEPARTMENT OF THE AIR FORCE
WASHINGTON

SPECIAL ORDER   9 September 1965
GB-249

DP, FIRST LIEUTENANT ROBERT A ANDERSON, Air Service, Army of the United States,
is awarded the Purple Heart for wounds incurred as a direct result of an act of
an enemy on 27 Aug 18.

BY ORDER OF THE SECRETARY OF THE AIR FORCE:

                                    J. P. McCONNELL, General, U.S. Air Force
                                    Chief of Staff

R J PUGH, Colonel, USAF   DISTRIBUTION:
Director of Administrative Services   GO

*First Lieutanant Anderson, shown at right in a
formal portrait, finally got his Purple Heart Medal
for wounds received in action. It came 46 years late,
having been overlooked in the confusion of the
winding down of the war.*

CHAPTER 18

The decade of the sixties was a dangerous, twisting time that is perhaps most well remembered for its violence. The assassinations of President Kennedy and his brother, Robert, and of Martin Luther King, Jr., Malcolm X, and Medgar Evers cast a pall over the nation. The Vietnam War divided the country as no other war had ever done, and all-out nuclear war loomed as a possibility because of the Cuban missile crisis. In the fiasco of the Bay of Pigs, the United States failed to overthrow Cuba's Fidel Castro. In a further diminution of American prestige, the Russians put Cosmonaut Yuri Gagarin in space, beating the Americans handily.

In the islands the population had reached more than sixty thousand, and for the first time, a million visitors poured out of the new jet-powered aircraft and spread out across Hawai'i. Large cranes loomed over downtown Honolulu and Waikīkī—cynics called them the "state bird."

Alex watched it all from the vantage point of years. But within his own company, there was also evolution and change. The year 1965 marked the one hundredth anniversary of Alexander Young's arrival in Hawai'i, and it was also the year in which Alexander Young's partner—Alex's uncle Conrad Von Hamm—died at the age of ninety-five. His obituary in the Honolulu Star Bulletin referred to the Von Hamm-Young Company as "a multi-million-dollar diversified operation and a moving force in Hawai'i's business life." Alex had been an integral part of that company—in 1925 he started out as a director; in 1927 he became treasurer; in the middle of the war years, 1942, he was promoted to vice president, and two years later he became president. In 1959 he reached the pinnacle of the company and was named the company's chairman. In 1968, at the age of seventy-four, he

Alex with James Pell (standing) and Conrad Von Hamm, who hired Alex away from his position in Chicago. He also was Alex's uncle by marriage.

was chairman emeritus. His situation, it seemed, was secure. But the majority of Von Hamm-Young's stock was publicly traded, and a local businessman, Randy Crossley, and others from an insurance company called the American Pacific Group, suddenly owned 52 percent of the company. It was enough to get Crossley a seat on the company's board of directors, where conflicts developed between Crossley and George Freitas, then chairman of Von Hamm-Young. Freitas quit in disgust in 1968, and Crossley became head of the company, which was renamed the Hawai'i Corporation.

Despite the changes that occurred, Alex never spoke disparagingly of the man who seemed to have taken the company by storm. "His remarks absout Randy Crossley were always optimistic," Pam Anderson remembers, "optimistic that Crossley would do good things for the company, and that eventually The Hawai'i Corporation would go on the New York Stock Exchange. That was the goal."

But in December 1973 the company went bankrupt. By that time Alex had retired, and with his health still good, he was enjoying golf and other pleasures. Fortunate to have other income, Alex weathered the financial readjustment. The advancing years had done little to stem his activity or to decrease his honors. When he retired in 1969 he was showered with congratulatory letters.

He was becoming something of an elder statesman by now. He was a director of the Bishop Trust Company and a member of the Royal Hawaiian Band Advisory Council; he was even made an honorary corporal by the commander of the U.S. Army in Hawai'i.

As he watched the islands change, he noted changes in music—in styles and technique, even in subject matter. While some of his contemporaries may have deplored the new music, Alex took it in stride. He enjoyed all kinds of music—the classics, country, even rock. His own songs were fewer now, for he began to have problems with his vision. He had always written his own manuscripts, and his diminishing vision, while never critical to his mobility, began to slow his music writing. But he never felt isolated from it, and throughout the decades from the 1930s through the 1960s and beyond, his music was played at home and abroad. He may have known that it would live beyond him.

The year 1970 brought sadness to Alex and his family. In April of that year, Paul Winslow died at a community hospital on California's Monterey Peninsula. His obituary identified him as a key official of the Del Monte Properties Company for four decades and recounted his service in two world wars. Alex would always remember him as a close friend whom he was happy to have as his brother-in-law, and he undoubtedly let his mind drift back to the day when Paul married his sister, Ruth, in a lovely wedding at Central Union Church.

Alex projected an air of humility and gratitude as the honors kept coming in. A story by Traylor Mercer in a local newspaper recalled how Anderson, Ward Kinney, Richard Kimball, Walter Dudley Child, Sr., and Sewell Turner had decided to form the Hawai'i Hotel Association. The Men's Club of Temple Emanu-El presented Alex with the Brotherhood Award for being "Hawai'i's ambassador of good will." The Quiet Birdmen gave him an award of honor on old-timers' night. To his great pleasure, the Rotary Foundation of Rotary International named him a Paul Harris Fellow "in appreciation of tangible and significant assistance in furthering better relations and understanding among peoples of the world." A letter from President Gerald Ford thanked Alex for his generous support.

The music world also continued its accolades. On March 15, 1975, the Honolulu Symphony—which Alex and Peggy had long supported and of which Alex had served as president for five years—honored Alex for his service and his accomplishments. At the Mayor's Symphony Ball,

Businessman Ben Dillingham was the emcee for a testimonial honoring Alex in 1963; it was one of many such honors Alex received throughout his long life.

Honolulu's then-mayor Frank Fasi presented Alex with a proclamation, but equally important in Alex's eyes was the evening of his music performed by leading entertainers. The symphony itself opened with a medley of his songs. Hilo Hattie performed, once again, the hula to "Cockeyed Mayor of Kaunakakai." Alfred Apaka sang "Malihini Mele," and Charles K. L. Davis performed "I'll Weave a Lei of Stars for You." There were performances by Ed Kenney, Beverly Noa, and Emma Veary, among others. By the time the evening ended with the entire company performing "I Will Remember You," Alex was overcome with emotion.

In an event a few years earlier Alex had been part of a similar program far from Hawai'i. It was at the Salt Palace Arena in Salt Lake City, Utah, on a warm July night in 1970, when Eugene Jelesnik conducted the Salt Lake Philharmonic in a program called "Days of '47." Alex was invited to take part in the program and did so by conducting his composition "That's Patriotic."

Never equating aging with a numerical figure, Alex went on with his life with purpose and activity. Nor was Alex afraid of controversy, and in 1973 he took on a local newspaper. On September 28 the *Honolulu Star-*

June 6, 1978

Dear Andy:

Sorry as the Cockeyed Mayor that I can not be with you to kiss you 84 happy times. Please realize that I know you helped me in my career more than anyone, and I am grateful. Happy Birthday you wonderful person. Keep young, keep smiling and keep writing our songs. I love you.

Hilo Hattie

Hilo Hattie P.O. BOX 207, HONOLULU, HAWAII 96810

Hilo Hattie was a good friend and admirer of Alex.
Her celebrated hula to his "Cockeyed Mayor of Kaunakakai" was always a show-stopper.

Bulletin had editorialized that there seemed to be no great support for maintaining the Waikīkī War Memorial Natatorium. The newspaper really stirred Alex's wrath when it went on to say:

> When it was built, it was to be a "living memorial" to the heroes of World War I. That war has now slipped 55 years into history and the world it was supposed to make safe for democracy seems no better now that it was then. Indeed, after the long Vietnam struggle, the American mood is one of utter war weariness and, after Watergate, disenchantment with its political leaders. . . . the people have become too cynical to make heroes of soldiers or self-serving politicians. . . . Whether the memorials to the builders will be more substantial than the memorials to war "heroes" is questionable—people today are too busy with their affairs to care much about history. . . . But future historians will deal more kindly with us if our heroes are builders, not destroyers.

Alex bridled at the use of quotation marks around the word "heroes" and took it as a jab at the military in general, for whom he had a long and profound respect. His letter back to the newspaper pulled no punches:

> The lead editorial in the Friday *Star-Bulletin* disturbs me considerably. Ostensibly about the Waikīkī War memorial Natatorium it develops into a slur against "war heroes" and particularly WW I "heroes," that war apparently too far back to be considered at all important. It also sounds off against all and sundry to do with the military.
>
> Having been born in that nebulous past before patriotism, discipline and prayers in school went out of style, I cherish the memory of many who answered the call as I did, and fell in battle in WW I. I was fortunate to return. My buddies and thousands like them who made the supreme sacrifice deserve to have their names enshrined forever. Whether in the Natatorium is relatively unimportant but to wipe out that record without substituting another suitable place is to me unthinkable.
>
> The other target of the editorial is the military. Memorials to Goethes, Curies, Salks and Leonardos by all means, and come the millennium maybe we won't need the military, but as long as

there are crackpots around who are able to rise to power through the support of a rabid following, unwatched and unchecked by a somnolent majority, there will be no substitute for a strong military posture and readiness for any eventuality.

World Wars I and II may not have "made the world safe for democracy" but I hate to think what our fate might have been if either had been won by the aggressor. Free Press would now be a figment of the imagination. So if this editorial was not intended to discredit the military and in particular to influence the thinking of our younger people in that direction, I urge that another look be taken and the need recognized for honoring and keeping green the memory of those who have done battle for their country. War heroes every one.

Fourteen years later the Natatorium was still around, and Alex had the satisfaction of writing a song about it called "The Waikīkī Natatorium Comes Alive": "In the memory of our heroes who died in the First World War, / Each name is here for all to see, enshrined forevermore." No one who remembered Alex's response to the editorial doubted that he worked the word "heroes" into his song with deliberation.

Alex never sought controversy. "He was an even keel sort of person," Pam Anderson has said, and her brother Leith referred to his father as "a quiet, gentle, caring man." But Alex did not turn from what he felt should be accomplished, as his attack on five German fighters in World War I demonstrated. One cause in which he fought a valiant, but losing, battle centered around the historic downtown Honolulu landmark built by and named for his grandfather, the Alexander Young Hotel.

The hotel was many things to many people. Primarily it was the leading hotel in Hawai'i before World War II, and in some of the suites lived people who were, or would become, famous in the islands. One notable tenant was Madge Tennant. Mrs. Tennant won renown for her paintings of Hawaiians, and she is one of a handful of local artists who gained worldwide recognition and respect. Visitors to the hotel included generals and war correspondents, including Ernie Pyle, on their way to or from the war. USO entertainers who made their temporary home at the Alexander Young included Maurice Evans and Judith Anderson.

World War II dealt kindly with the hotel; when the Pacific Fleet and military installations in Hawai'i were attacked on December 7, 1941, the closest damage to the hotel was a block away on King Street, where the roof was damaged on the Lewers and Cooke hardware store. Local people had feared that the hotel would be a prime target in any attack because it housed officers of the local naval intelligence unit and some Army engineers.

Honolulu residents remembered the tea dances, the candy shop where chocolate-covered macadamia nuts were born, the bakery, the elegant lobby, the coffee shop, and the restaurant. The hotel also served as offices for many in medical professions, especially dentists.

Modern times caught up with the hotel, in spite of its memories and its historic importance. By 1980 Bishop Street had lost half of the buildings it had in 1930, with only four of the original structures standing, including the Alexander Young. The demand for office space downtown was outpacing the available units. By July 1980 the owners of the building, Milwaukee's Northwestern Mutual Life Insurance Company, applied for a demolition permit. The fact that the building was on the Hawai'i Register of Historic Places meant only that the owners were required to file three months' notice with the state. At the time when the owners filed, the hotel had 125 office tenants, having ceased to operate as a hotel ten years earlier.

When word got out that the hotel was going to be torn down, there was a public outcry. At least twelve thousand people signed a petition to save the old building, which had maintained its strong structure over the years. Old-timers remembered that the hotel had set the standards in size and scope for buildings that followed; that it had, in fact, been the beginning of Bishop Street.

Alex waded in with a local newspaper article deploring the planned demolition. He pointed out that it was the first hotel of any consequence in the islands and one of the finest west of Chicago. He also speculated that his grandfather Alexander Young, instead of demolishing such a historic building, would devise a way to save it—and do so at a handsome profit.

Alex's efforts, and the wishes of others who wanted to save the building, were futile. Despite protests that went on for more than a year, demolition began on July 7, 1981, and by early autumn the building was gone. It was replaced by two tall towers and the one-acre Tamarind Park. It is safe to say that although many older residents may appreciate the new look at Bishop and King Streets, the memory of the storied old hotel will remain as a bittersweet recollection.

CHAPTER 19

On an April morning in 1980 Alex received a note from his physician, Dr. Harry Arnold. A pathology report, Arnold wrote, showed that Alex's three lesions—on his left arm, under his chin, and on the right side of his neck— were skin cancer, and they all needed to be removed. The good news, wrote Arnold, was that all were considered a low-grade malignancy, and if they were completely removed, they should cause no further trouble.

Alex was then two months shy of his eighty-sixth birthday, and the pathology report certainly was cause for reflection. He could have been forgiven if the skin cancer had been enough to induce a quiet surrender to time, but he maintained a keen interest in watching his children and grand-children achieve their own successes, and he decided to fight back. He had the lesions treated at California's Long Beach General Hospital in a new procedure called hypothermia that was not yet available in the islands. It was a three-day treatment for which Alex was placed under general anesthesia while surgeons placed radioactive material in the lesions and focused on them with microwaves. Five days later the material was removed. The lesions became smaller and smaller and gradually disappeared. Alex's only public complaint about his condition was an observation to an interviewer in 1984: "As a kid in high school I did a lot of surfing. I'd go out almost every afternoon and weekend and surf. And as a result . . . I've got a hell of a skin condition today. We didn't know in those days that you had to protect your skin. Didn't have any of those screens. So I've got that bad part of it. But I always enjoyed the water." Most photographs taken of Anderson from this period show him wearing a hat as protection against the sun.

He was pleased that while everyone knew his age nobody paid much

Peggy and Alex celebrated Peggy's 90th birthday at the Outrigger Canoe Club, where Peggy's brother, Dad Center, created the Club's swim team.

attention to it, except for to honor him on his birthday. His creativity stayed reasonably high. Only a few years earlier he had written a song in commemoration of the Wai'alae Country Club's fiftieth anniversary, and he wrote the theme song for the March 30, 1985, Miss Deaf Hawai'i pageant at the Princess Kaiulani Hotel. With his attitude and work ethic he was never an old man to anyone who knew him, and he kept his sense of humor, a trait he and Peggy shared.

But the years were taking their toll on Peggy, who was only a year younger than Alex. She could recall events of the past but had difficulty with day-to-day events; her doctors thought she might be suffering from Alzheimer's. Pam Anderson remembers the closing days:

> I was living in San Francisco for a while and was transferred here, so I lived nearby for eight to ten years. Then their housekeeper retired, so I came in to help. Mother gradually went further down in health, so I stayed on, just happened to be in the right place at

the right time. I had the opportunity to spend the last part of their lives with them, and it was interesting, and at times very humorous. They just had a good sense of humor and made light of things that were difficult. They were very courageous people.

Peggy and Alex had Carmen Lucero to help take care of them. Pam remembers her as someone "with a great rapport . . . she would read to them, get their breakfast, spend the day driving them. We were very fortunate to have her, and she took wonderful care of them." Alex, Pam remembers, was very upbeat and encouraging in the face of illness. "He was very comforting and they were always together."

Eventually the family hired nurses to come in and relieve Carmen. The night nurse was sleeping one night when Pam got up to check on her mother. Peggy had died in her sleep. It was September 11, 1990. Peggy had lived ninety-five years.

Alex was saddened but stoic. He understood that it was time for Peggy to go, and that his own time could not be far off. That night he looked back in memory over a happy marriage that had lasted seventy-one years, and he knew how fortunate he had been.

Both the Andersons could age gracefully,
as evidenced by this 1987 Christmas card.

For thirty-five years Alex was a member of the Bohemian Club, an exclusive all-male group of more than two thousand members with a San Francisco headquarters. He had attended, without fail and into his nineties, the club's annual encampment at the Bohemian Grove in Monte Rio, California, on the Russian River. At these encampments Alex played and sang his songs and took part in musical programs before both small and large audiences.

The club was made up of high achievers, including some big-name performers. During one of the encampments in the woods, Alex was in charge of a musical built around his song "I Dream of Bohemia." Two of his costars were Randy Crossley and William F. Quinn, who was the last appointed governor of the territory and the first elected governor of the state of Hawai'i. Such luminaries as Bing Crosby, Ray Bolger, Art Linkletter, and Edgar Bergen pronounced the show a "smash hit."

Club rules prohibited bringing the same guest to the encampment on consecutive years, so Alex alternated taking his sons. Allen remembers the encampments:

> This is a two-and-a-half-week outing in the club's huge redwood forest in very luxurious camping facilities, with appropriate hired help. It consists of excellent gourmet "feedings" out under the stars, continuous musical and other entertainment put on by the club members, many of whom are well-known professionals. There are stage plays, with men playing the parts of both sexes, music and plays written by members, and the orchestra and actors are all members.

Dad's annual contribution and one of the reasons he was so well known throughout, was about a fifteen-minute performance playing and singing his songs. This was always well received, with cries of "encore." He had glee club training at Cornell during his college days, and his voice was still respectable well into his nineties. He accompanied himself on 'ukulele.

He invited me to attend as his guest in July 1969, when I was in Napa; the grove is only about fifty miles from there. I took my clarinet and saxophone and accompanied him on clarinet when he performed. This pleased him greatly because it relieved much of the strain associated with a solo performance. The fact that I know all of his songs and the way he sings them helped. We were in great demand, being invited to perform at several

Alex, sitting second from left, and his cohorts at the Bohemian Club in San Francisco. The membership was exclusive and the purpose was fun.

member gatherings during the two-week plus outing. I remember thinking, "What a ham he is when he's on stage. He loves it."

After my permanent return to Honolulu in 1973, he wanted to repeat the process as often as we could, and we did, both privately—that is, among friends—and publicly a few times. Since Bohemian Club rules disallowed the same guest attending in consecutive years, he invited me every other year for several years.

By 1983 Allen had decided that these performances were worth preserving:

> With the help of Bud Dant, a Bohemian friend of Dad's and mine, retired vice president of Decca Records, and resident of Kailua-Kona, we made plans to record him professionally with professional Hawaiian backing, i.e., steel guitar, 'ukulele, guitar, bass. The initial recording was done in Honolulu on 24-track tape.
>
> Then [we went] to Hollywood with the tape for the final dubbing down by Bud and the Chief Engineer at Warner Brothers. That produced a very acceptable master tape of him playing and singing thirteen of his best-known tunes, with pure Hawaiian accompaniment. This didn't quite satisfy my requirements… so I went back to Warner Brothers a short while later and played an accompanying track on clarinet, which was dubbed in to make a side two on the cassette. Side one is thirteen tunes pure, side two is the same thirteen songs with the clarinet added. Following that we did the act many different times and places. As his partying and other things slowed down, the act slowly went into mothballs, which was all right with me, because we got it on commercial-quality tape at or near its peak.

The cassette cover showed Alex wearing a lei. A review of the cassette in the *Honolulu Advertiser* said that the cassette was "a lot of music with a lot of unpretentious sentiment." It continued:

> At 90, Anderson is not much of a singer—but the voice is as comfortable as a back-porch rocker with as many squeaks in the laid-back appeal. The thing that comes through on this record-

At one of Alex's birthday parties — and he had many because of a legion of friends — he shares a moment at the microphone with daughter Pamela.

PRESIDENT BILL CLINTON
Honorary National Chairman, American Red Cross

Martin D. Schiller
Chairman of the Board
Hawaii State Chapter

Kathryn Bennett
Executive Director
Hawaii State Chapter

1994 HUMANITARIAN AWARD DINNER

Honorary Co-Chairpersons
Joan Bellinger
Joan Bickson

Chairperson
Jane B. Tatibouet

Vice-Chairpersons
Claire W. Engle
Dr. David A. Ramsour

Committee Members
James Andrasick
Russell W Alger
Dr. John Henry Felix
Sue T. Inouye
Warren K. K. Luke
June Reinwald
Murray Towill

Coordinators
Carmella Hernandez
Julie Ahue Murray

The 1994 Red Cross Humanitarian Awards Dinner honored Alex and singer Danny Kaleikini, one of many honors both men received.

ing is his obvious love and aloha for the Hawai'i that has been home to him for years.

Thus the cassette is somewhat of a document of what Hawaiians and Mainlanders have been singing and feeling and thinking about the Isles for years . . . a lifetime of song has been assembled here—and while oodles of other versions of these titles have been previously immortalized by others, Anderson finally gets in his very special licks.

At age ninety Alex received the Sidney A. Grayson Award from the Hawai'i Academy of Recording Artists, for his outstanding contributions to Hawaiian music. The award, which was named for the founder of KCCN Radio, was later renamed the Lifetime Achievement Award and evolved into the annual and much-respected Nā Hōkū Hanohano Awards.

In 1992 Alex received an honor that took him all the way back to his roots—and no doubt evoked memories of Turnberry and Ayr and his old squadron. Hawai'i's Caledonian Society, a group of some three hundred people of Scots ancestry or Scottish connections, voted Alex the Scot of the Year and honored him as such at the Robert Burns dinner on January 25, 1992, at the Ilikai Hotel. It was no small achievement in a place where, on a per capita basis, it is reported that there are more people of Scots ancestry than any other place outside of Scotland (the statistic immediately raises doubts and protests, but the key is the per capita basis).

Yet another honor was one that he shared with the popular entertainer Danny Kaleikini in 1994, when they received the Humanitarian Award from the Red Cross. Just a year later, Kaleikini was present at Alex's one hundredth birthday party, and he told all present that "in all my travels around the world, the song that is most requested is 'Lovely Hula Hands.'"

Alex settled into a comfortable routine, which his son Allen remembers well:

It included lunch each weekday except other of his clubs—Outrigger, Pacific Club, Wai'alae, or Rotary at the Royal Hawaiian Hotel. Pam either joined him or left him to join the old men's table. I decided to ask him to join me on Wednesdays at the

Outrigger, my club. He accepted . . . we had lunch every Wednesday right up to the Wednesday before he passed away.

After a while the breezes at the Outrigger bothered his eyes, so we went to the Wai'alae in the enclosed men's grill. We talked about one of two things usually, either computers, about which I had become very literate, or old times, such as his childhood. His long-term memory was sharp as a tack, because of his photographic memory. I can remember some days when I would start things by asking a question about his childhood, and an hour later we had finished lunch . . . and the story.

Sometimes Allen would begin a lunch conversation by telling Alex about some new development in computer sciences, and each time Alex would wish he'd been born thirty years later so he could have gotten into the computer field. "He listened with complete attention," Allen said, "because he, like me because of him, was a gadget man. He was a mechanical engineer by formal education, and new technology—mechanical, electronic, or whatever—intrigued him." It was, perhaps, one of the secrets of his long life—this ability to maintain awareness, to keep pace with the advancements around him. Another secret may have been his remarkable athletic ability, which went all the way back to his Punahou days when he ran track and played football.

The ending, when it came, was a gentle one. When he was ninety-eight Alex began to need blood transfusions every couple of weeks. His body wasn't producing enough blood cells, and because of his age it was deemed best to avoid invasive surgery. He was still mobile for his age, and his memory was still intact. He was robust enough to appear on a radio show around his 100th birthday and to make what proved to be a final appearance at Bohemian Grove. The family agreed, however, that it was time to provide nursing support, so a nurse was hired to stay in the home at Mākālei Place.

There came the day when Bob, having spent the night at the home, was leaving as Pam arrived. Just as Pam entered the house the nurse called, "Come quickly, your father's going." Pam went up to stay with him as he was taking his last breaths, and he went peacefully. It was Memorial Day, May 30, 1995, one week short of Alex's 101st birthday.

"It was hard . . . very difficult," Pam recalls. "But they both wanted to live out their lives in the house, and fortunately they were able to do that."

The funeral was the kind of island service that would have warmed Alex's heart. Warm tributes were given by close friends, and the music no doubt would have stirred him to join in.

Already, the newspapers were celebrating his achievements and his long life. The *Honolulu Advertiser* editorialized, in part: "Those old-time songs presented an image of a happy Hawai'i, where cultures blended in music and a good laugh was an important part of every occasion. One man who did as much as anyone to create that image, that feeling, was R. Alex Anderson, who died yesterday at age 100 . . . no one can deny his love for these Islands and his enormous contributions."

The *Honolulu Star-Bulletin* quoted a longtime family friend and expert on territory-era music, Harry B. Soria, Jr.: "Basically, he's the godfather of hapa-haole music." The newspaper also quoted the late Tono Todaro's book, *Golden Years of Hawaiian Entertainment,* in which Todaro wrote, "I like to think that Alex and his lovely Peggy were born for each other—and I cannot think of another couple that have spent a more glorious lifetime of singing together, enjoying life together, and sharing and caring together for the betterment of their community and all mankind."

Irmgard Aluli, herself a musical and cultural icon in Hawai'i, said, "What comes to mind is that I'm thankful Hawai'i had Alexander Anderson. I feel he will be long remembered for the beautiful music he composed . . . his songs show his love for Hawai'i, its beauty, its romance and its people . . . I'll always treasure these songs that he left behind. I feel he's a kind, gentle person and a true *kama'āina.*"

The funeral, held at Saint Andrew's Cathedral, drew loving tributes from family and friends. Danny Kaleikini was there, telling how Alex's music had made Hawai'i known around the world. Punahou's Rod McPhee spoke of Alex's "great sense of humor" and of how "he leaves a void in our community which will never be filled . . . but that is no cause for despair. Rather, we must be thankful that he passed our way and that we had the opportunity to know him." He added that Alex's songs "will be sung as long as there is a Hawai'i."

Many performers turned out to pay tribute, including Pua Mana, Arthur Lyman, Ed Kenney, Nina Rapozo, and Irmgard Aluli. Overhead, a vintage aircraft flew in remembrance of Alex's heroics in World War I, and there were Masonic and military honors. At graveside services in O'ahu Cemetery a lone bagpiper played a funeral dirge, and the strange, keening music of the pipes flowed clearly in the slight wind. Perhaps at

CHAPTER 20

that moment many were recalling one of Alex's most poignant and un-forgettable songs, "I Will Remember You":

I will remember you, in the silent and lonely night.
And the memory of your smile will bring me back the light;
I will remember you, when the leaves lie upon the ground,
With the memory of a kiss, a kiss in Summer found . . .
When the winds of Winter come crying through the darkness,
Your lovely voice will come to me,
Even though in spirit, across the miles that part us,
Crying, I love you.

CHAPTER 21

Alex was a man who loved many—his family, friends, buddies lost in the war, and associates in his many organizations and clubs. With a love that shimmered in every song, he loved Hawai'i's beauties and culture, its mixture of races, and its sunlit days and romantic nights. The songs he wrote were not composed for his own amusement; he wanted to give them to the islands and the island people. Under different circumstances he might have devoted his life only to writing music, because it was his way of expressing an emotion so large that the islands themselves could not contain it. As Rod McPhee observed at Alex's funeral services, his music will be around as long as Hawai'i lasts.

His music arrived at exactly the right time in Hawai'i's development. His songs were sung and danced from the 1930s through the next six decades, and they will continue to be played. His songs appear in classic collections, on compact discs, and in the performances of entertainers across the state. Royalty checks still arrive from all over the world, including Cairo, Tokyo, the Pacific Islands, Norway, and the British Isles. For many a potential visitor the music weaves a spell, creating an image of a place they hope to find as romantic as the songs.

Posthumously, Alex's music continued to earn honors. On March 26, 1998, Governor Benjamin Cayetano proclaimed the day to be Hawaiian Music Hall of Fame Day. At a concert that evening produced by Kahauanu Lake, five musicians were honored with induction into the hall of fame. They were David Nape, Bina Mossman, John Almeida, Irmgard Aluli, and R. Alexander Anderson. At the nineteenth annual Nā Hōkū Hanohano Awards of the Hawai'i Academy of Recording Artists, which took place on May 15, 1996, at the Sheraton Waikiki Hotel, Alex received a newly created lifetime-achievement award from the American Society of Composers, Authors, and Publishers, the prestigious and influential organization in which Alex held membership for fifty-six years, from 1939 until his death. Pam Anderson proudly accepted the award on her father's behalf.

The classic photo of Alex, with his ʻukulele and red carnation lei.

When an individual lives so long and performs so well, it is fair to ask the question—what is his legacy? What difference did he make in the community?

For Alex's family—he left four children, thirteen grandchildren, and thirteen great-grandchildren—his legacy is the memory of a prominent man that they share with the community, a musical icon whose songs are likely to outlive even the youngest of the great-grandchildren. It is also a sense of family, of closeness and support even in disagreements, with more than a hint of Scots clannishness.

For the community, Alex's legacy is one of an astonishing unselfishness. Alex gave his time, energy, and acumen to an extraordinary number of causes. When there was a need to revitalize downtown Honolulu, Alex was there heading up the Downtown Improvement Association. When it was apparent in 1945 that Hawai'i would need to promote tourism vigorously, he joined up with the Hawai'i Visitors Bureau. When the need for a Hawai'i hotel association became obvious, Alex helped get it underway. Lē'ahi Hospital might have languished without his vigorous support. His efforts on behalf of aviation in Hawai'i resulted in modernization of some airfields, and he also helped to set safety standards. He always supported the military, for he had firsthand knowledge of what it takes to preserve a nation's safety from outside aggression.

He gave generous support to his fraternities and the Punahou and Cornell alumni associations. He was a loyal Mason all his life. He brought leadership to entities as diverse as the Pepe'ekeo Sugar Company and the Honolulu Symphony Society, and he loved the Rotary and supported it throughout his life. He was not a "sunshine soldier" either; when he signed on with an organization he stayed with it as long as he was needed, as his fifty-six years in ASCAP and his long memberships in the American Legion and the Rotary demonstrated.

But long after his World War I exploits are forgotten by all except family and curious historians, and long after his stewardship of Von Hamm-Young Company will have faded from memory, it is his music that will remain.

Harry B. Soria, Jr., has been quoted as calling Alex a foremost composer of *hapa haole* music and saying that Alex was "by far the most Hawaiian, because his songs tell of the flowers and the Islands and the people, and don't get hung up on being cute and novel little ditties. He's into rhyme and all those things, and his music is very commercial but at the same time there's a sophistication to it, and a warmth that local residents identify with." Soria singles out "Haole Hula"—which was Alex's own favorite—as the song that

says it all about the feeling here…it's English, but it embodies the love of nature the way the Hawaiian [language] songs do. It was eloquently talking about the skies and the breeze and ocean and the dancing from a real *kamaʻāina* perspective…it was like his autobiography, how being born in Hawaiʻi but being Caucasian could still be special….A lot of hapa haole music sounds dated, but Andy's music will still be performed well after the millennium. It's aged well, and it's a reflection of the depth of the man.

Alex put all his great emotion for Hawaiʻi in Haole Hula, writing that "in every note I'll tell of the spell of my Islands." And it was true.

Alex was "a good musician," according to Bobby Evans, a musician and keen observer of the Hawai'i music scene. "He could read music, but mostly he knew notes and could follow. And he could write—he's going to forever be at the top of the great hapahaole composers, and he had more success with his songs than the others; even today, most tapes you pick up have at least one Anderson song on them."

Later in life Alex often sat down to play with other musicians, and when he faltered at times it was because of his vision, which grew worse over the years. This meant he sometimes went into the wrong key because he could not see the notes that well, but he always recovered quickly. In staying active in music for such a long time, Alex inspired other musicians, and this, too, is part of his legacy. He brought an honesty to his music; he never tried to write in Hawaiian because, as Evans points out, "It's not an easy language, and haole can't write it well."

In his last days, perhaps even in his last hours, Alex may have let his mind drift back to the summer days of his youth, which were filled with innocence and the joys of Hawai'i that were so beautiful as to be sublime. He may have thought of the fresh-faced and talented girl he had married, and who had accompanied him for more than seventy years in that most challenging of partnerships, marriage. He may have remembered the skies over France and his perilous trek across Belgium to freedom. Then there were the decades after the war, when his life returned to normalcy in counterpoint to the changes taking place in Hawai'i.

Music had accompanied him throughout his life, and eventually his great love for the islands and its people became inseparable from his music. At the very end music may have brought him comfort, for he knew that all he had done and been, and everything he sang and wrote, came from a joyful heart.

*Alex and Peggy together as always; it was
a marriage that lasted seventy-one years.*

FROM A JOYFUL HEART

Appendix A

Songs by R. Alexander Anderson

R. Alexander Anderson wrote upwards of two hundred songs, not all of which were published, and some of the published ones were not copyrighted until long after their composition. He wrote songs for specific events that were performed but not necessarily published; although these songs enlivened many local occasions, they are now only remembered by few. That Alex spent time and talent writing such music, knowing it would not earn him any returns, is an example of his generous nature.

Probably the best-known collection of his published songs is contained in a songbook from 1971 called "R. Alexander Anderson's Famous Songs of Hawai'i," published by Bibo Music Publishers. The listing that follows is from that songbook. Songs are listed by title, composer(s), and copyright date, but it is important to note that the copyright dates do not necessarily indicate the years that songs were written. "OC's Team," for example, was written when Anderson was at Punahou, but it was not copyrighted until 1949. Similarly, "Alohaland" was written when Anderson was at Cornell University between 1912and 1916, but it carries a copyright date of 1925.

Songs Published by R. Alexander Anderson, 1925–71:

"Alohaland," Anderson, 1925
"Lei, Lei, Buy Lei," Anderson and Don Blanding, 1928
"Haole Hula," Anderson, 1928
"Honeymoon Isle," Anderson and Flora J. Center, 1929
"Malihini Mele," Anderson, 1934
"Soft Green Seas," Anderson and Leonie Weeks, 1934
"Reach Up and Pick a Star," Anderson, 1934
"The Cockeyed Mayor of Kaunakakai," Anderson, 1935
"Red 'Ōpū," Anderson, 1935
"Love Song in the Night," Anderson and George Hopkins, 1936
"When Twilight Falls," Anderson, 1936
"On a Coconut Island," Anderson, 1936

"The Cockeyed Daughter (of the Cockeyed Mayor)," Anderson, 1939

"I Had to Lova and Leava on the Lava," Anderson, 1939

"White Ginger Blossoms," Anderson, 1939

"Lovely Hula Hands," Anderson, 1940

"Two Shadows on the Sand," Anderson and Norman Burlingame, 1940

"Blue Lei," Anderson and Milton Beamer, 1940

"I Will Remember You," Anderson and Carter Nott, 1941

"No Tears," Anderson, 1943

"They Couldn't Take Ni'ihau Nohow," Anderson, 1943

"Moonlight," Anderson, 1946

"I'll Weave a Lei of Stars for You," Anderson and Jack Owens, 1948

"Mele Kalikimaka," Anderson, 1949

"OC's Team," Anderson, 1949

"'Sunshine'—The Beach Boy," Anderson, Francis Cummings, and Frances Ah Chong, 1951

"Right on the Kinipōpō," Anderson, 1952

"Mu'umu'u Māmā," Anderson, Fred T. Smith, and Peter Lee Zoellner, 1953

"Holiday Hula," Anderson, 1954

"Aloha Malihini," Anderson and Don McDiarmid, 1955

"Have I Kissed You Lately?" Anderson, 1955

"Hula Rock," Anderson, 1956

"Coral Reefs," Anderson, 1956

"Just an Orchid from Hawai'i," Anderson, 1957

"There Are Two Eyes in Hawai'i," Anderson, Al Hoffman, and Dick Manning, 1957

"Have You Seen a Malihini Do the Hula?" Anderson, 1957

"My Dream," Anderson and Jack Ackerman, 1957

"Sailing With You in Hawai'i," Anderson, 1957

"Kā'anapali," Anderson, 1957

"Kona Moon," Anderson, 1957

"Poi for Two," Anderson, Fred T. Smith, and Peter Lee Zoellner, 1958

"Narcissus Queen," Anderson, 1958

"Cherry Blossoms," Anderson, 1958

"Moonlight on Diamond Head," Anderson, 1959

"Hawai'i U.S.A.," Anderson, Fred T. Smith, and Peter Lee Zoellner, 1959

"Jungle Rain," Anderson and David M. Kupele, 1959

"Aloha Is the Spirit of Hawai'i," Anderson, Fred T. Smith, and Peter Lee Zoellner, 1960

"Music of Guitars," Anderson, 1960

"Christmas in Hawai'i," Anderson, 1961

"Island Love Song," Anderson, 1962

"Back in Alohaland," Anderson and Jack Owens, 1963

"Spring Spends the Winter in Hawai'i," Anderson and Don McDiarmid, 1964

"Old Kāhala," Anderson, 1964

"Hawai'i Nei," Anderson and Charles Hale, 1964

"Skies over Hawai'i," Anderson, 1965

"Moon of Mauna Kea," Anderson, 1965

"The Air Force Deb," Anderson and Sybil Webber, 1965

"How Can She Shake So Little So Much?" Anderson, 1965

"The Army Debutante Waltz," Anderson, 1965

"Hawai'i Smiles," Anderson, 1965

"'Ukulele Isle," Anderson and Herbert Ohta, 1966

"What a Day (Nō Ka Best)," Anderson, 1966

"Santa's Hula," Anderson, 1967

"Waste Time Watch the Hands," Anderson, 1968

"That's What America Is All About," Anderson, J. A. Stebbins, and Ed Kenney, 1968

"Big Brown Eyes," Anderson, 1969

"Rock, Rock, Rocket to the Moon," Anderson, 1969

"Take Me Back to Honolulu," Anderson, 1970

"I'm from Honolulu," Anderson, 1970

"The Sea, the Sky, and the Mountains," Anderson, 1970

"Rainbow 'Round the Moon," Anderson, 1970

"Maybe It Could Be for Real," Anderson, 1970

"Share Your Blessings," Anderson and W. A. Dillon, 1970

"My Three Dimensional You," Anderson, 1971

"Our Last Hawaiian Moon," Anderson, 1971

"Moon Don't Make a Monkey Out of Me," Anderson, 1971

"Lovely Flowers of the Evening," Anderson, 1971

"Go Punahou," Anderson, 1971

"Honolulu Honeymoon," Anderson, 1971

"Billy Goat Strut," Anderson, 1971

"I'll Sing You a Song of Hawai'i," Anderson, 1971

"Up Tight Baby," Anderson and Charles Bud Dant, 1971

"Remember I Gave My Aloha," Anderson, 1971

Affiliations of R. Alexander Anderson

R. Alexander Anderson was a familiar name to many who served on boards or commissions related to community affairs in Hawai'i during the past several decades, for Anderson was involved with so many of these organizations at various times. He also took part in the leadership events and activities of a number of private clubs that he joined simply for the fun of it. Following is a list of his major affiliations:

American Legion
ASCAP (American Society of Composers, Authors, and Publishers)
Bishop Trust Company
Bohemian Club
Commercial Club—president
Downtown Improvement Association—a founding member, later president
Eta Kappa Nu, engineering society
Hawai'i Aeronautics Commission
Hawai'i Hotel Association—a founding member
Hawai'i Employers Council
Hawai'i Visitors Bureau—chairman
Honolulu Chamber of Commerce—director
Honolulu Rotary—president, later district governor of Rotary International
Honolulu Symphony Society—president for five years, lifetime member
Kani Ka Pila
Lē'ahi Hospital—trustee
Loge le Progrès de l'Oceanie
Mid-Pac Country Club—a founding member
O'ahu Country Club
O'ahu Development Conference
Order of the Daedalians
Pacific Club
Pearl Harbor Yacht Club—commodore
Pepe'ekeo Sugar Company

Pi Kappa Alpha fraternity, Cornell University
Punahou Alumni Association
"QB" (Quiet Birdmen)
Red Cross—chairman, 1953 fund drive
Territorial Aeronautics Commission
200 Club
U.S. Army Advisory Committee
Wai'alae Country Club—a founding member
Waikīkī Yacht Club

Selected Bibliography

Many salient facts of this biography are contained in the private papers of Robert Alexander Anderson as retained by his daughter, Pamela Susan Anderson. Some are undated, others are illegible in places, but all reflect Alex Anderson's life and times and music. The author has drawn heavily on these papers to fashion a picture of an extraordinary man. Some other sources are noted:

Ames, Kenneth L. *On Bishop Street*. Honolulu: First Hawaiian Bank, 1996.

Anderson, R. Alexander, and Margaret Leith Center Anderson. Interview by Pauline King Joerger, in connection with a Punahou anniversary survey. February 2, 1976.

Anderson, R. Alexander. "Shot with Luck." *McClure's*, August 1919–February 1920.

Berger, John. "Interview." *Hawai'i*, August 1995.

Brown, DeSoto. *Hawai'i Goes to War*. Honolulu: Editions Limited, 1989.

Daws, Gavan. *Shoal of Time*. Honolulu: University of Hawai'i Press, 1968.

Day, A. Grove. *History Makers of Hawai'i*. Honolulu: Mutual Publishing, 1984.

Dwyer, Matthew L. Private papers. In *Who We Are* , March 1991.

Finlayson, Iain. *The Scots*. New York: Atheneum, 1987.

Glasebook Foundation for Preservation of Military Aviation History. *American Aviators in the Great War, 1914–1918*. Carson City, Nev.: Glasebook Foundation for Preservation of Military Aviation History, 1984.

Harvey, Edmund H., et al. *Our Glorious Century*. New York and Montreal: Reader's Digest, 1998.

Honolulu Advertiser, June 21 1929; June 14, 1959; April 28, 1963; October 31, 1965; March 16, 1976.

Honolulu Star-Bulletin, June 21, 1929; September 28, 1973; February 29, 1975.

Letters, variously dated or undated, from: Lowell Thomas, Cole Porter, Mary Pickford, Admiral Chester W. Nimitz, Arthur Godfrey, Andy Williams, Lawrence Welk, Andre Kostelanetz, General Victor Krulak, Patricia Nixon, President Richard Nixon, Admiral John S. McCain, Jr., and Odette Gilbert.

National Red Cross. Letter. Washington, D.C., October 24, 1918.

Prange, Gordon W. *At Dawn We Slept*. New York: McGraw-Hill Book Company, 1981.

Pukui, Mary Kawena, and Samuel H. Elbert. *Hawaiian Dictionary*. Honolulu: University of Hawai'i Press, 1986.

Skywriter, June 3, 1966.

Stephan, John J. *Hawai'i under the Rising Sun*. Honolulu: University of Hawai'i Press, 1984.

Trager, James. *The People's Chronology*. New York: Henry Holt and Company, 1992.

United Press, November 9, 1918. Story by Don Chamberlain.

Vestey, Pamela. *Melba*. Melbourne: Phoebe Publishing, 1996.

War Department. Adjutant General's Office. Letter. Washington, D.C., October 17, 1918.

ABOUT THE AUTHOR

Scott C. S. Stone has been Navy officer, foreign correspondent, newspaperman and national prize-winning novelist and film-writer. Some of his books are centered in Asia, where he has lived and worked. He is a combat veteran of both the Korean War and the fighting in Vietnam. Research has taken him from the roof of Norway to the South Pole, from the lagoon of Bora Bora to Yugoslavia and beyond. He always comes home to Hawai'i, where he has maintained a home for more than forty years.

Also by Scott C. S. Stone

Fiction

The Coasts of War
A Share of Honor
The Dragon's Eye*
Spies
Song of the Wolf
Scimitar
The Dragon Legacy
The Chinese Robe

Nonfiction

Pearl Harbor, The Way It Was
A Study in Counter-Insurgency
Volcano!!
Wrapped in the Wind's Shawl (with John E. McGowan)
Land of Fire and Snow
Honolulu: Heart of Hawai'i
The Essential Guide to Maui
The Essential Guide to the Big Island
The Story of C. Brewer
Infamy and Aftermath
The Island of Hawai'i / from Sail to Space
He Mele O Hawai'i (A Song of Hawai'i)
The Last Battleship
Blueback
Living Treasures of Hawai'i
The Tsunami of 1946 and 1960 (with Walt Dudley)

*Edgar Award, Mystery Writers of America

176